BABY-LED FEEDING

BABY-LED FEEDING

A Natural Way to Raise Happy, Independent Eaters

Jenna Helwig

with Natalia Stasenko, MS, RD

HOUGHTON MIFFLIN HARCOURT • BOSTON • NEW YORK • 2018

For information about permission to reproduce selections from
this book, write to trade.permissions@hmhco.com or to Permissions,
Houghton Mifflin Harcourt Publishing Company, 3 Park Avenue,
19th Floor, New York, New York 10016.

hmhco.com

Library of Congress Cataloging-in-Publication Data is available.

ISBN 978-0-544-96340-5 (paperback); 978-0-544-96342-9 (ebook)

Book design by Alissa Faden

Printed in China

TOP 10 9 8 7 6 5 4 3 2 1

To my parents, with
boundless love and gratitude

CONTENTS

INTRODUCTION

Baby-food makers, blenders, itsy-bitsy jars of mashed foods, batch cooking, and puréeing. What if I said you could skip all of that in favor of a more natural, flavor-filled, and family-friendly transition to solids? Welcome to baby-led feeding.

There are so many milestones with a new baby—smiling, sitting up, sleeping through the night (hooray!)—but one of the most exciting and rewarding is when a baby begins her transition to solid foods. Watching her take her first bites is like a little miracle. She's being introduced to a wonderful world of flavor, initiated into a human act that will hopefully bring her sustenance and joy her entire life. It all begins with the first bites in the high chair.

Until a few years ago, the mainstream strategy for introducing solids was clear: Start spoon-feeding thin purées between 4 and 6 months, gradually thicken the texture, then make it lumpier, and finally introduce finger foods. Foods were bland, devoid of big flavor that might be considered "challenging" to a baby's palate.

But times have changed. Both the flavor and texture of baby foods have been given an upgrade, thanks to recent evidence highlighting the importance of a quick progression between textures and an early exposure to a variety of tastes. Babies are now eating more complex, flavor-filled dishes than most of their grandparents or parents did when they were the same age.

Another recent change is the promotion of early self-feeding, a natural step toward fostering adventurousness and independence in babies. When I wrote *Real Baby Food* a few years ago, I recommended introducing finger foods along with purées when babies begin the transition to solid foods. Including finger foods in the diet from early on helps babies develop fine motor skills, sample new flavors, and become accustomed to varied textures. But purées were still the nutritional bedrock, at least for the first couple of months.

But since then, interest in early self-feeding, or baby-led weaning, as it is often called, has soared. New parents are curious about feeding their babies in this very tactile, family-friendly way.

Baby-Led Feeding is an easygoing, friendly guide to helping your baby become a happy, independent eater through self-feeding. The book covers all the nutritional bases, answers new parents' most pressing questions, and features easy, delicious recipes for the whole family to enjoy together.

WHAT IS BABY-LED FEEDING?

Baby-led *weaning* is a feeding method recently popularized in the United Kingdom that encourages skipping purées altogether when transitioning babies to solids. There is no buying jars or pouches of baby food or blitzing roasted chicken in the food processor. Instead, babies are allowed to explore, get messy, eat what they can, and set their own pace.

So why is this book called Baby-Led *Feeding*? First off, *weaning* is a confusing term. Here in the United States, it means transitioning babies off breastmilk or formula. In fact, for at least the first six months of eating solids, babies should still be drinking plenty of one or the other.

Second, advocates of baby-led weaning sometimes recommend a very strict approach in what should be a very happy, fun, flexible time. They say that if a single purée passes your baby's lips, you have failed at baby-led weaning, or that what you're doing really isn't baby-led weaning. If you offer your child a pouch on a particularly busy morning, you've blown it and should revert back to only breastmilk or formula for a couple of weeks before starting finger foods again. To me, this seems unnecessarily restrictive and likely to cause more—rather than less—stress.

Baby-led feeding (BLF) is a more flexible, practical approach. Yes, by all means make finger foods the dominant or even exclusive source of solid foods for your baby. But there are good reasons why you may want to offer your baby purées as well, and that's just fine, too. The key is baby-led. When you offer your child finger foods, she decides how much she wants to eat. She picks up the food and puts it in her mouth. If you are spoon-feeding your child, you pay close attention to her cues. Is her mouth open, ready to receive the food? If so, great, feed away. But if her mouth is closed or she's distracted or upset, stop. Follow her lead. Even though she's a baby, she decides if and how much she eats.

THE ADVANTAGES OF BABY-LED FEEDING

Although there isn't a lot of research available on self-feeding yet, many experts agree that one of the main benefits of self-feeding is greater satiety responsiveness, the mechanism that allows us to eat until we are full and stop before eating too much. This may lead to better health and weight outcomes in the future.

Another positive outcome is a boost in oral motor development. Research shows that a majority of six-month-olds are able to reach out and grasp food. By offering babies finger foods, parents are providing important opportunities to practice these skills in a developmentally appropriate way.

Additionally, early self-feeding seems to help reduce the risk for picky or fussy eating behaviors in older children. There is more research needed to officially declare this connection, but using finger foods and encouraging self-feeding often means exposure to a greater variety of food, including family

WHY HAS BLF BECOME SUCH A POPULAR WAY TO FEED BABIES?

Parents who have tried it rave that it promotes:

Early integration into family meals, since babies can eat modified versions of what their parents and siblings eat from the very beginning.

Baby's recognition of and reliance on their own hunger cues. With BLF there is no pressure for baby to take "just one more bite." This may help promote more mindful eating in the future.

Happier mealtimes. With BLF there is no pressure . . . babies eat as much as they want and have fun exploring color, taste, and texture while they're at it.

A generally healthy diet, since there is a heavy emphasis on fruits, vegetables, and other whole foods.

A more traditional, "natural" way to feed babies. After all, our ancestors didn't open up jars of bland food and coax spoonful after spoonful into their babies' mouths.

An openness to a variety of foods and less choosiness as babies grow up.

Acceptance of more interesting and varied flavors and textures, since babies aren't just eating sweet purée after sweet purée.

Faster development of fine motor skills.

Less stress on parents and caregivers, since fewer special baby-only meals need to be prepared.

favorites and traditional ethnic dishes.

Finally, baby-led feeding is fun! Babies join in family meals from an earlier age, enjoying the first steps of their eating journey, exploring and learning with every bite.

HOW TO USE THIS BOOK

So if baby-led feeding is all about babies eating "regular" family foods, why have a cookbook at all?

One of the key features of this book is the visual guide at the beginning of chapters two and three. These photos show parents and caregivers the safest ways to cut and cook single-ingredient foods for babies feeding themselves. It's natural to have a lot of questions about what's safe and what isn't, and this book addresses the most common sources of confusion.

And while parents can strive to eat together as often as possible, it is rarely practical to do so three meals a day. Modern moms and dads will often want to serve their babies a separate breakfast and may need to send lunch along to daycare or Grandma's house. The recipes in this book meet all those needs.

Chapter one is packed with information on starting solids, infant nutrition, equipping your kitchen, recommended ingredients, and answers to frequently asked questions.

Chapter two is for beginning self-feeders, around ages six to eight months. The photo gallery at the beginning of the chapter illustrates how to cut foods for babies still only able to grasp foods with their whole palms. Appealing but basic recipes offer ideas for other nutrient-rich foods like Simple Poached Salmon (page 50), Basic Baked Oatmeal (page 55), and Cinnamon-Banana Pancakes (page 60). Recipes include tips for making foods like roasted carrots and avocado less slippery for babies still working on their motor skills.

Chapter three features recipes and ideas for more advanced self-feeders, around age eight months and up. Around this time most babies develop their pincer grasp, the ability to pick up smaller pieces of food with their fingers and thumbs. The photos in this chapter offer guidance for appropriate single-ingredient finger foods at this more advanced stage. The recipes in this chapter are heartier and more adventurous as well. Babies will love Pumpkin Pie Pops (page 118), Zucchini Bread Waffles (page 124), Sweet Potato Hummus (page 98), and Green Apple–Spinach Smoothies (page 114).

Chapter four is full of family recipes. These are dinner dishes that are ideal for the entire family, including baby. The texture is appropriate for beginning eaters, the spice level is reasonable, and, most important, the recipes are full of flavor to satisfy everyone, including your adventurous baby. No bland foods here!

ABOUT US

As a children's nutrition and feeding expert, trained chef, and a mom, I am incredibly passionate about giving children the best nutritional start in life. For me, that includes feeding children healthy foods, of course. But even more important, it's about helping a child develop a happy relationship with healthy foods. One of my favorite things about baby-led feeding is that it encourages that relationship. Natalia Stasenko is a registered dietitian and the mother of three daughters. She practiced baby-led feeding with her youngest daughter. Her nutritional expertise and real-world experience help make this book a thorough resource for new parents.

ABOUT THE ICONS

 30 Minutes or Less—The recipes marked with this symbol can be ready in under a half hour, start to finish.

 Freezer-Friendly—Making food ahead of time or storing leftovers in the freezer can be a boon for busy families. The recipes with the snowflake symbol keep well in the freezer for up to three months. For best results, defrost the food overnight in the fridge, or defrost in the microwave. Never leave frozen food on the counter to defrost for more than one hour.

a note on nutrition

The recipes in this book all feature nutritional information, but it's helpful to know approximately how many calories and nutrients babies need on a daily basis. Remember, babies will still get much of their nutrition from breastmilk and formula. These numbers are just benchmarks. Don't worry if your baby doesn't hit all these numbers on a daily basis.

	6–12 months
Calories	600 to 900
Protein	11g
Calcium	260mg
Iron	11mg
Potassium	700mg
Vitamin C	50mg
Vitamin A	2000IU

chapter one

BABY-LED FEEDING

Let's Get Started

WHEN TO START

Simple: when *your* baby is ready.

It's good to keep in mind official recommendations, but they can be confusing. The American Academy of Pediatrics (AAP) recommends parents be guided by their baby's developmental readiness when considering starting solids, and attempt to breastfeed exclusively for about six months. The organization does not provide any guidance for formula-fed babies. The American Academy of Allergy, Asthma & Immunology says solids may be started between four and six months, and the UK-based baby-led weaning movement suggests starting finger foods at six months and skipping purées altogether.

Your baby is probably ready to begin his solid food adventure when he can sit up with support, when he is able to hold his head and neck still, and when he loses the thrust instinct and his tongue no longer pushes food out of his mouth.

For me, the most important sign that my baby was ready to start solids was that she was downright fascinated with food. She looked at my plate greedily when I was eating, and she even tried to grab what I was feeding myself.

If you're starting with finger foods, as opposed to purées, you'll probably want to wait until your baby is close to six months old.

Then he'll be better able to feed himself and will become less frustrated with the process. If you're interested in starting with purées, your baby may be ready a month or more before that.

Remember that every child is different. Don't be alarmed if your baby is still uninterested in food at six months. Just wait a week or two and try again.

It's a bit counterintuitive, but when you're first starting solids, it's best to feed your baby solids when he's not overly hungry. If he's famished, he may get easily frustrated if he's having difficulty self-feeding or even ingesting enough purée to take the edge off. Instead, offer him solids between breastmilk or formula feedings, so he isn't overly hungry or overly full. Also, make sure he isn't ready for a nap, or you'll likely have a fussy eater on your hands.

HOW TO START

It is very important to offer your baby food when he is seated upright, not lying down or even leaning back. If he can't quite sit up without support in a high chair, it's okay to tuck a few rolled-up dishtowels around him.

If you're beginning with finger foods, start by placing a couple of pieces of one food on his tray.

If you're starting with a purée, always make sure you have your baby's attention before putting food into his mouth. No sneaking in bites! Baby-led feeding is about following your baby's lead, regardless of whether you're spoon-feeding or he's eating finger foods.

Whether it's finger foods or purées, let your baby decide how much food he wants to eat. Once he gets distracted or closes his mouth tight or throws all his food on the floor, mealtime is over. Don't worry if he hasn't eaten all his food. The early days of feeding are about exploration, and mealtime should be a fun experience for your baby, not a stressful one.

WHAT TO START WITH

Unlike the old days, when parents gave their babies rice cereal to start, today there are no hard-and-fast rules about what foods to begin with. So feel free to start with fruits, vegetables, grains, or even meats. Any of the foods in chapter two are good candidates for first foods.

In the early days of eating solids, finger foods should be cut into a length and width about the size of your pinky, since most babies starting finger foods will grasp foods with their whole palm. When babies are older, about eight months or so, they will develop a pincer grasp and be able to pick up smaller pieces of food with their fingers and thumb. In either shape, the food should be soft enough that you can mash it with gentle pressure from your thumb and forefinger. And ideally it isn't too slippery

for your baby to get hold of!

While it's tempting to stick with just fruits and vegetables, try to incorporate sources of important nutrients like iron, zinc, and omega-3 fatty acids into your baby's first foods, especially if you are breastfeeding, since formula is fortified with these nutrients. See the chart on page 24 for more details.

the no-no list

Not a lot of foods are off limits for your baby's first meals, but these are:

- Honey. Since this sweet substance may be tainted with botulism, skip it until your baby is 12 months old.
- Choking hazards such as popcorn, hard candies, whole nuts, and big globs of sticky nut butters. Avoid these foods until your child is four years old.

Allergy Rules

For many years, pediatricians and allergy experts recommended delaying the introduction of allergenic foods like peanuts, tree nuts, and eggs until babies were older, in the hopes of staving off food allergies. In fact, that approach appears to be counterproductive, and now most experts believe that introducing allergenic foods early—between four and ten months—may help protect against allergies.

The traditional introduction of solids calls for introducing single-ingredient foods one at a time to make sure it's easy to identify the culprit if there's an allergic reaction. But with baby-led weaning as it's often practiced—with baby simply eating family meals—that approach is more challenging. After all, not many family meals are composed of only one ingredient!

Natalia and I believe that it's still safest to introduce foods one by one, at least for the first month or two. New foods can be introduced as finger foods or as purées, but this period gives your baby a chance to adjust to solid foods and gives you the opportunity to make sure your baby doesn't suffer from food allergies.

Introduce new foods at home and in the morning so you or your child's caregiver have a full day of being with your baby to notice allergic reactions. Avoid introducing two new foods simultaneously. Some experts recommend waiting a full three days before introducing new foods. In most cases, this is extreme. Wait a day or two and then move on to the next new food. Remember, during this period the more flavors you can introduce to your baby, the better!

Once your baby has tried some of the most allergenic foods and hasn't had a reaction, you can begin serving mixed meals.

In the end, it's your choice how to introduce foods to your baby—one at a time or mixed from the beginning. Either way, be vigilant for signs of allergic reaction.

these foods are the most highly allergenic:

- Peanuts
- Tree Nuts
- Soy
- Fish
- Shellfish
- Eggs
- Dairy
- Wheat

In general, there's no need to wait to introduce these foods to your baby. But if your child is at high risk for food allergies (if he suffers from eczema or if close relatives have food allergies) or you have any questions about when to introduce particular foods, speak with your pediatrician.

 *evaluate*
THE SYMPTOMS

MILD SYMPTOMS
INCLUDE

- Hives
- Eczema
- Redness of the skin around the eyes
- Stomach pain
- Sneezing
- A dry cough
- Nausea or vomiting
- Diarrhea
- Itchy mouth

If you notice mild symptoms, stop serving the food and speak with your pediatrician.

SEVERE SYMPTOMS
INCLUDE

- Swelling of lips, tongue, or throat
- Difficulty swallowing
- Shortness of breath
- Turning blue
- A drop in blood pressure
- Loss of consciousness
- Chest pain
- A weak pulse

If your baby exhibits a severe symptom, call 911 or get to the nearest emergency room right away.

Daily Feeding Schedule and Suggested Portion Sizes

It's helpful to have a guideline for when and how much to feed your baby. But don't be alarmed if your baby eats more or less than these suggestions. All babies are different, and yours might be especially hungry one week and less so the next. As long as your baby is gaining weight normally, just follow his lead.

Cereal amounts are included in the chart in case you're including spoon-feeding in your baby's diet. If not, stick with the other serving suggestions. Since most babies are not able to self-feed before six months of age, serving sizes of fruit, vegetable, and protein purées are included in tablespoons for babies ages four to six months.

one serving

PROTEIN	GRAIN	FRUIT OR VEGETABLE	DAIRY
¼ egg, 2 thin strips of chicken, ½ meatball, 1 ounce fish, or 2 tablespoons purée. Good protein choices include meat, fish, poultry, eggs, tofu, or beans and lentils.	½ cup oatmeal or cooked rice, quinoa, pasta, or couscous; 2 slices baked oatmeal; or ½ slice toast, cut into sticks.	2 pieces, such as 2 slices of soft pear or steamed apple, 2 steamed carrot sticks, ¼ medium avocado, 2 small steamed broccoli florets, or 2 tablespoons purée.	½ cup (4 ounces) full-fat yogurt; ¾ ounce full-fat cheese, shredded or cut into thin sticks. Cow's milk is not recommended as a main drink for infants under 12 months.

	4 TO 6 MONTHS	6 TO 8 MONTHS	8 TO 10 MONTHS	10 TO 12 MONTHS
FIRST THING IN THE MORNING	Breastmilk on demand or 6–7 ounces formula	Breastmilk on demand or 6–7 ounces formula	Breastmilk on demand or 6 ounces formula	Breastmilk on demand or 6 ounces formula
BREAKFAST	1–2 tablespoons cereal 1–2 tablespoons fruit or vegetable	2–4 tablespoons cereal, or ½–1 serving grain 1–2 servings fruit or vegetable	4–6 tablespoons cereal or 1–2 servings grain 1–2 servings fruit or vegetable	4–6 tablespoons cereal or 1–2 servings grain 2 servings fruit or vegetable
MIDMORNING	Breastmilk on demand or 6–7 ounces formula	Breastmilk on demand or 6–7 ounces formula	Breastmilk on demand or 6 ounces formula	1 serving dairy and 1 serving fruit or vegetable
LUNCH	1–2 tablespoons cereal 1–2 tablespoons fruit or vegetable OR Breastmilk on demand or 6–7 ounces formula	1–2 servings fruit or vegetables ½–1 serving grain Breastmilk on demand or 6–7 ounces formula	1–2 servings protein 1–2 servings fruit or vegetable 1 serving grain 1 serving dairy Breastmilk on demand or 6 ounces formula	1–2 servings protein 1–2 servings fruit or vegetable 1 serving grain Breastmilk on demand or 6 ounces formula
MIDAFTERNOON	Breastmilk on demand or 6–7 ounces formula	Breastmilk on demand or 6–7 ounces formula or 1 serving dairy	1–2 servings fruit or vegetable 1 serving grain or 1 serving dairy	1–2 servings fruit or vegetable 1 serving grain or 1 serving dairy
DINNER	Breastmilk on demand or 6–7 ounces formula	½–1 serving protein 1–2 servings fruit or vegetable ½–1 serving grain	1–2 servings protein 1–2 servings fruit or vegetable 1 serving grain	1–2 servings protein 2 servings fruit or vegetable 1 serving grain
BEFORE BED	Breastmilk on demand or 6–7 ounces formula	Breastmilk on demand or 6–7 ounces formula	Breastmilk on demand or 6 ounces formula	Breastmilk on demand or 6 ounces formula

Important Nutrients
for Babies

If your baby eats a wide variety of fruits, vegetables, grains, and proteins supplemented by breast-milk or formula, chances are, he'll be getting all the nutrition he needs to grow healthy and strong. But there are a few crucial nutrients that are worth paying special attention to, either because of how important they are to your baby's development or because the recommended daily amount can be a challenge to reach. The chart on page 24 highlights foods rich in these nutrients.

IRON allows blood cells to carry oxygen to muscles and organs and is very important for brain development in small children. At periods of rapid growth, like infancy and childhood, our iron needs increase. To ensure your baby is getting enough iron, offer at least two iron-rich foods each day.

ZINC is crucial for proper growth and a strong immune system. Our bodies cannot store zinc effectively, so we need a consistent supply via dietary sources.

BOTH IRON AND ZINC, quite luckily, share common food sources, including meat, vegetables, and fortified breakfast cereals. This is one of the reasons experts now recommend introducing meat into babies' diets early on; the human body absorbs iron and zinc from meat more easily than it does from non-meat sources. Formula is fortified with iron and zinc, but if your baby is breastfed, it is important to make sure that his diet includes solid-food sources of these nutrients by nine months of age.

OMEGA-3 FATTY ACIDS.

DHA (docosahexae-noic acid) is a type of omega-3 fatty acid that serves as a key structural component of cell membranes. Recent research has also connected DHA to optimal retinal and brain development, especially during pregnancy and the first 24 months of life. Some DHA is found in breastmilk, and certain formulas are fortified with this important nutrient, but the best dietary sources of DHA are fatty fish and DHA-enriched eggs. Fish and shellfish that are lower in mercury are safer for your baby, so opt for salmon, pollock, trout, catfish, canned light tuna, and shrimp over shark, swordfish, and king mackerel.

ALA (alpha-linolenic acid) is a type of omega-3 found in plant foods, such as nuts, seeds, and leafy greens. Although our bodies can convert ALA into DHA, the conversion rate is neither efficient nor reliable. That's why DHA supplementation is usually recommended for vegan babies who do not drink DHA-fortified formula.

VITAMIN D

plays a vital role in calcium absorption and immunity. It is also related to a lower risk of numerous chronic and auto-immune conditions, from type 2 diabetes to heart disease. While research is still unlocking the potential of this powerful nutrient, it is clear that its dietary sources are quite sparse. If your baby is not getting a lot of sunlight or is dark-skinned, make sure to discuss supplementation with your doctor.

AND DON'T FORGET ABOUT FAT.

Neither total nor saturated fats should be restricted in the first year of life. In fact, both are very important for satiety, vitamin absorption, and brain development. To ensure that your baby gets enough, avoid low-fat dairy in the first year and add olive oil or butter to foods you prepare.

Recommended Daily Amounts for Babies

IRON (11MG)	ZINC (3MG)	OMEGA-3 DHA (100–150MG) OR ALA (300–500MG)	VITAMIN D (400IU)	TOTAL FAT (30G)
Breakfast cereal, fortified with 100% DV for iron, 1 serving (check the label for serving size)—18mg	Beef, cooked, 3 ounces—7mg	Salmon, wild, cooked, 1 ounce—235mg DHA	Salmon, wild, cooked, 1 ounce—149IU	Breastmilk, 8 ounces—11g
Tofu, raw, regular, ¼ cup—3.3mg	Breakfast cereal, fortified with 25% DV for zinc, ¾ cup serving—3.8mg	DHA-enriched eggs, 1—up to 150mg DHA	Orange juice, fortified with vitamin D, 1 cup—137IU	Full-fat cheddar cheese, 1 ounce—9g
Lentils, boiled and drained, ½ cup—3mg	Pork chop, cooked, 3 ounces—2.9mg	Sardines, canned in oil, drained, 1 ounce—144mg DHA	Milk, vitamin D-fortified, 1 cup—115–124IU	Full-fat yogurt, 8 ounces—8g
Beef, cooked, 3 ounces—2mg	Chicken, dark meat, cooked, 3 ounces—2.4mg	Tuna, light, canned in water, drained, 1 ounce—63mg DHA	Soy milk, fortified with vitamin D, 1 cup—100IU	Peanut butter, 1 tablespoon—8g
Chicken, cooked, 3 ounces—1mg	Chickpeas, cooked, ½ cup—1.3mg	Cod, cooked, 1 ounce—42mg DHA	Yogurt, fortified with 20% DV for vitamin D—80IU	Avocado, ¼—6g
Raisins, seedless, ¼ cup—1mg	Egg, 1 large—0.6mg	Fortified milk, 8 ounces—16mg DHA	Tuna, canned in water, drained, 1 ounce—51IU	Olive oil, 1 teaspoon—4.5g
Egg, 1 large—0.8mg	Green peas, frozen, cooked, ½ cup—0.5mg	Flaxseeds, ground, 1 teaspoon—570mg ALA	Egg, 1 large (vitamin D is found in yolk)—41IU	Egg, boiled, 1 large—5g
Broccoli, boiled and drained, ½ cup—1mg	Peanut butter, 1 tablespoon—0.5mg	Kale, cooked, ½ cup—67mg ALA	Breakfast cereal, fortified with 10% DV for vitamin D, 1 cup—40IU	Butter, 1 teaspoon—4g

Nutrient amounts in specific foods are approximate. Values vary based on origin of the food, cut of meat, and brand.

Kitchen Tools

One of the beauties of BLF is that you don't need any special equipment beyond your usual kitchen arsenal. You can skip buying any special baby-food makers (even if you plan on feeding your child purées) and cook up all kinds of deliciousness with basic kitchen tools.

The Essentials

- Cutting boards, at least one large
- Chef's knife and paring knife
- Whisk
- 1–2 wooden spoons
- 1–2 rubber spatulas
- Spatula
- Tongs
- Ladle
- Kitchen shears

- 1–2 large baking sheets
- Medium saucepan (3½ quart)
- Large saucepan with lid (5 quart or 8 quart)
- Steamer basket
- Colander
- Small and large mixing bowls
- Small nonstick skillet
- Large skillet

- Blender
- Box grater
- Standard and mini-muffin tins
- 9 x 13-inch baking dish
- 8 x 8-inch baking dish
- Measuring cups and spoons
- Vegetable peeler
- Instant-read thermometer

The Extras

- Food processor
- Microplane grater
- Waffle iron
- Stand mixer
- Stovetop griddle

- Slow cooker or multicooker
- Wire cooling rack
- Rolling pin
- Loaf pans
- Pie plate

- Cake pans
- Citrus squeezer/reamer
- Spiralizer
- Kitchen scale

The one item on the Extras list that I highly, highly recommend is a food processor. Its uses are so varied and the amount of work it can save you is so enormous that I think it's worth the investment. When I finally bought a food processor, I couldn't believe it had taken me so long.

Ingredients

Even when they're eating the same foods as the rest of the family, babies have some special needs. Keep this information in mind as you plan your baby's meals.

BREASTMILK AND FORMULA

Until a baby turns one, breastmilk or formula will continue to make up a large portion of his diet. This is especially true for babies who self-feed, since they may not actually ingest as much food as babies who are spoon-fed. See the portion chart on page 21, but know that formula needs vary. Some babies prefer to drink more formula less often, or less formula more frequently. Pay attention to your baby's hunger cues when he's bottle-feeding to make sure he's eating only as much as he is hungry for.

Typically, after the introduction of solids most babies need around 32 ounces of formula a day, broken up into four or five feedings. At around eight to ten months, as your baby gets the hang of feeding himself and solid snacks are introduced, the amount of formula your baby needs will drop to 24 to 28 ounces, broken up into three to five feedings. See the chart on page 21 for more details.

If your baby is breastfeeding, continue to let him drink until he has had his fill.

GOING ORGANIC

As parents, we want to give our babies the very best, and buying organic food can feel like a no-brainer. Conventionally grown foods contain a higher concentration of pesticides, and pesticides accumulate more quickly in our babies' little bodies.

That said, most research suggests that the pesticide levels in conventional food are safe, and organic food can be costlier—especially when a lot of it ends up on the floor as your baby feeds himself! If you're committed to offering your baby organic food but concerned about the expense, consider only buying organic versions of the foods that are the most contaminated. The Environmental Working

Group (EWG) tracks the "dirtiest" and "cleanest" fruits and veggies in terms of pesticide load (although even most of the "dirtiest" produce has pesticide levels under the maximum limits established by the federal government). You can find those lists at ewg.org.

Another strategy, and the one I use in my house, is to choose organic for the foods we eat the most often. For my family, that's milk, eggs, berries, and baby spinach. I also strive to buy meat and poultry that are either organic or raised without the use of antibiotics and artificial growth hormones.

If the expense puts some foods out of reach or you're just not convinced of the benefits, don't feel guilty about skipping going organic. The most important thing is to feed your family a wide variety of colorful fruits and vegetables, along with lean proteins, however they're grown and raised.

DAIRY

Before age one, babies should not drink cow's milk, since it can be hard to digest and inhibit iron absorption, leaving little room for other nutritious foods in your baby's small tummy. Instead, stick with breastmilk or formula. Beginning at 12 months, your baby can transition to full-fat cow's milk, and at age two, you can switch to reduced or low-fat milk, if you prefer.

It's perfectly okay, though, to offer your baby full-fat yogurt (made with cow's milk) and cheese as part of his meals and to use full-fat milk in baking and cooking from about six months.

SUGAR

Avoid giving your baby added sugars during her first year. (In fact, the American Heart Association recommends no added sugars for the first two years of life.) This includes maple syrup and especially honey, which can contain botulism.

That said, my philosophy is that if a family meal contains a bit of sugar for balance or maple syrup for a hint of sweetness, that's fine. Just skip the desserts, presweetened cereals and yogurts, and sugary beverages for baby.

SALT

One of my first lessons in culinary school was the importance of salt for adding flavor to food. Pitting a plain steamed broccoli floret against a lightly salted one is nowhere near a fair fight. And frankly, it makes adults and children much more likely to eat a healthy portion of broccoli. For most people, a sprinkle of salt takes food from blah to bliss.

For babies, though, too much sodium can put stress on their kidneys. So when making food just for your baby, skip the salt shaker. When making family meals for BLF, some parents choose to add a tiny bit of salt, or just salt grownups' and bigger kids' food at the table. The recipes in the First Foods and Heartier Finger Foods chapters don't call for any salt. For those recipes that you might want to continue making as your baby grows up, a salt measurement is included in the Age It Up description.

The Family Meals chapter includes a salt measurement in each recipe as an optional ingredient. (The nutritional information for each recipe does not include optional ingredients.) My hope is that you'll continue to make these recipes long after your baby is a toddler, and you'll likely want to include salt in the recipes then for top flavor.

FRESH FROM THE FREEZER

Don't automatically shun canned and frozen foods. When rinsed, low-sodium canned beans and lentils (from BPA-free cans) make nutritious foods for baby. Frozen foods, especially, are a great option. Since frozen fruits and vegetables are picked and frozen at the height of freshness, they are just as nutrient-packed as their fresh counterparts. My frozen favorites include cooked chopped spinach (such a timesaver!), berries, cherries, and mango.

BIG FLAVOR

Don't shy away from adding herbs, spices, and other pops of flavor like citrus and savory cheeses to your baby's food. There's no evidence that babies prefer bland foods, and the more flavors they try now, the greater the chances they'll like more foods later. Avoid spicy (as in hot spicy) foods; add chiles and other fiery foods in small amounts when your baby is closer to a year old.

COOKING

As I said in my previous book *Real Baby Food*, while your baby is in taste-training, you are in kitchen-training. Whether you're an avid cook or a struggling beginner, the more you cook, the more comfortable you'll be in the kitchen, and the healthier and more delicious your family's meals will become. Just like eating, people aren't born knowing how to cook. With time and experience, cooking will become a skill that will serve you and your family well for years to come.

Taste-Training

Before the age of one, most babies are more open to new flavors than they ever will be again in their lives. From kale to corn and salmon to sweet peas, this "flavor window" is the time for little ones to try it all. Many scientists now believe that children's taste preferences are established before they even learn to walk. A recent study suggested that babies who rarely consumed fruits and veggies rarely consumed them as older children, too. It follows that the more flavors your baby tries, the more likely he is to continue to eat them.

> ## BABIES DO NOT SPRING FROM THE WOMB EAGER TO EAT A BALANCED DIET FULL OF LEAFY GREENS. EATING WELL IS LEARNED.

Now, this doesn't mean if your child happily accepts kale as a nine-month-old, he will continue to relish it throughout his toddler years. Most children go through a sometimes years-long choosy phase beginning around age two and lasting until around age six. But children who ate kale as babies are more likely to come back around to it than children who did not.

Your baby may make a hilarious face the first time he tastes green beans or spinach, grimacing, spitting out the food, wrinkling his nose.

This is completely normal! It doesn't mean he will never like these foods. Keep putting them on his high chair tray. He will likely try them again and learn to enjoy them. Don't give up. Research shows that it can take up to a dozen tries for a child to accept a new flavor, and that number only goes up the older a child is. Children like foods that are familiar to them, so give them the chance to become accustomed.

On the flip side, never force or pressure your child to eat something he doesn't want. Your job is to offer healthy, tasty options in appropriate portions. His job is to decide what and how much he eats. Don't try to do his job.

It's worth repeating: "Don't give up." It's frustrating when your child rejects a food, especially if you have spent significant time preparing it. (Believe me, I know!) Rejected food seems wasteful and expensive, but please persevere. We don't expect our children to learn to read overnight, and we need to be just as patient as they learn to eat.

Babies do not spring from the womb eager to eat a balanced diet full of leafy greens. Eating well is learned. As Bee Wilson says in the illuminating book *First Bite: How We Learn to Eat*, "The way you teach a child to eat well is through example, enthusiasm, and patient exposure to good food."

Making the Case for a Mixed Approach

Some proponents of traditional baby-led weaning argue that serving purées alongside finger foods is confusing for children and may even be dangerous as babies are learning to handle two completely new textures at the same time.

However, there is no evidence that it is unwise to offer both textures simultaneously, providing babies are developmentally ready for solids and can pick up finger foods. In fact, a mixed approach—offering your baby both finger foods and purées—can be a convenient and less stressful way to prevent possible nutritional gaps while promoting the development of self-feeding skills and encouraging independence.

Here are six reasons why a mixed approach may make sense for your family:

1. VARIETY OF TEXTURES

The early introduction of safe finger foods allows babies to develop hand-eye coordination, practice grasping skills, and promote oral motor development. But spoon-feeding may also be important as it teaches a different set of skills, such as scooping the food off the spoon and manipulating it in the mouth before swallowing. Via both purées and finger foods babies get vital exposure to a variety of textures, which helps them become better eaters now and in the future.

2. PREVENTION OF NUTRITIONAL "GAPS"

Some babies may not be able to consume enough finger foods to get the nutrition—especially iron and zinc—they need. Feeding them purées rich in these nutrients can be an easy way to prevent nutritional imbalances.

3. LESS PRESSURE AND ANXIETY

Some babies prefer to start with finger foods, while others do better with purées for the first few weeks. The mixed approach helps reduce parental anxiety around gagging and choking. At the same time, its flexibility allows parents to stay attuned to their baby's developmental cues.

4. CONVENIENCE

However beneficial finger foods are, they can also be a messy and labor-intensive way to feed a baby, especially when traveling or on the go. The convenience of spoon-feeding purées may be what parents need from time to time in our busy world.

5. RESPONSIVE FEEDING

Both spoon-feeding and finger foods can be used to feed the baby in a responsive way, which helps babies stay attuned to their hunger-satiety and develop a healthy relationship with foods. The responsive feeding principle is more obvious when a baby self-feeds, since the baby chooses what—if anything—to put in his mouth. In order to spoon-feed a baby in a responsive way, parents should wait for a baby to pay attention before placing a spoon in her mouth, remain sensitive to her satiety signals, and allow the baby to determine the amount of food she wants to eat.

6. PREVENTION OF FOOD ALLERGIES

Recent research suggests that feeding babies potentially allergenic foods (eggs, dairy, peanuts, tree nuts, fish, seafood, wheat, and soy) at six months or earlier may help prevent food allergies in the future. The mixed approach allows for easy exposure to these foods in a convenient form of purée.

I've heard that "food before one is just for fun." Is that true?

Yes and no. When your baby is just starting solids, he is likely to be exploring and playing more than eating. As his eating skills develop, the portions of solid foods actually ingested will likely go up. The biggest shift often happens at around nine to ten months when most babies naturally reduce their intake of milk or formula and start getting more nutrients from solid foods. Some nutrients found in solid foods, such as iron and zinc, are especially important for development.

If I already started with purées, can I still switch to only feeding finger foods, or does that mean my baby is more likely to choke?

It is fine to switch. Babies are equipped with learning mechanisms that allow them to master a variety of textures from early on. Besides, serving your baby finger foods will contribute to the development of important oral motor skills, strengthen self-regulation, and make your life easier later down the road when she becomes a confident self-feeder.

Won't my baby choke if I give her finger foods before she has any teeth?

Babies are surprisingly powerful chewers even before their teeth come in, provided the food is tender. They are also equipped with a natural safety mechanism: the gag reflex. This can help ensure that foods that may cause choking are pushed forward in the mouth. It's a good (if scary, at times) system. By preparing your baby's food properly, you can make BLF much safer and minimize gagging. For more details on gagging and choking, see page 44.

My baby seems hungry, but he's having a hard time eating enough to satisfy him. What should I do?

The act of eating and especially self-feeding is hard work for babies. Besides, some babies need more calories than others, and their appetites vary greatly from day to day. The easiest way to make sure your baby is getting enough food is to allow him to eat as much solid food as he wants at regular mealtimes. It may be helpful to offer a variety of textures, including mashed or puréed foods, so he can keep improving his eating skills and also have an easier way to meet his caloric needs. Finally, allow him to drink as much breastmilk or formula as he wants at each feeding, especially if he is under ten months old, when most of his caloric needs are satisfied through drinking.

I don't think my baby actually eats much when she feeds herself—is that okay?

Whether with BLF or a traditional purée approach, few babies are able to consume large amounts of solid food right away. Their tummies are small, breastmilk or formula still provide most nutrition, and flavors of new foods can be overwhelming. When using the BLF approach, be prepared for your baby to actually eat a very small amount of food, since most of it ends up on the floor—and on your baby. That's one reason to consider offering your baby purées alongside finger foods, as it gives him the chance to learn self-feeding while still getting the important nutrition he needs.

Does my baby have a "virgin gut," and does that mean I can't feed him certain foods?

The idea that before six months of age babies have a "virgin" or "open" gut allowing big protein molecules and pathogens to escape directly into the bloodstream is a myth that may sound quite scary for some parents. In reality, intestinal permeability (or the ability of food particles to cross the intestinal lining) dramatically decreases in the very first days of life, so by the time your baby is ready for solid foods, his gut is far from being "virgin." The digestive system will keep maturing and adapting its enzyme production in response to the food that is on the menu, but it is a challenge human bodies are prepared for from about four months of age. So there is no need to avoid any food out of fear that it will damage your baby's gut.

How do I know if my baby has eaten enough?

This is an easy one! Just watch your baby carefully and she will give you plenty of cues. Losing interest in food, turning her head away, closing her mouth when the spoon approaches, or playing with finger foods instead of eating them are all signs of your baby getting full. If you try to push her to eat more, you will have a fussy baby spitting out food everywhere. So just trust her to know when she has had enough, and wind down the mealtime swiftly.

Is it true that giving a baby purées teaches them to swallow before learning to chew, and that BLF teaches a baby to chew, then swallow? Could that be a problem?

Since purées do not need to be chewed, babies can quickly get pretty good at eating them. The only skill they need is moving the food toward the back of the mouth in order to swallow it. Finger foods, on the other hand, are more challenging, because the food needs to be bitten off and chewed before it is ready for swallowing. Some babies can handle this additional challenge from the beginning, while others will spit out the food or gag and need more time to master finger foods.

Are there any babies who shouldn't try self-feeding?

Babies who were born prematurely or who have medical or developmental problems may have trouble with self-feeding at an early age. Talk with your doctor if you have questions. Also, if your baby gags frequently and is distressed by it, or if he vomits when exposed to certain foods or textures, take a step back to purées or the texture he comfortably tolerates and talk to your doctor about further oral motor and/or sensory assessment. But remember that some babies are just more cautious eaters without any underlying issues, and consequently don't have much interest in self-feeding or exploring foods. Offering a variety of textures and flavors in a responsive way will help your child look forward to mealtimes while expanding his variety at a comfortable pace.

10 RULES FOR BABY-LED FEEDING

1 Wash your baby's hands before mealtime.

2 Always make sure your baby is sitting up when he eats.

3 Never place finger foods in your baby's mouth for him.

4 Make sure finger foods are cut into safe shapes: adult-pinky-size for babies six to eight months old, chickpea-size for older babies.

5 Cook hard foods like apples and carrots until they're tender, but still hold their shape.

6 Skip most added sugar and salt in your baby's food.

7 Be sure to include sources of iron, zinc, and healthy fats in your baby's diet.

8 Always stay with your baby while he eats.

9 Be responsive, paying close attention to your baby's hunger cues. There's no pressure on a little one to take "just one more bite" or feeding in front of the TV to distract him into eating more food.

10 Don't be afraid to spoon-feed purées from time to time if you'd like.

chapter two

FIRST BITES

(6 months and up)

It's time! Your baby is able to sit up with support, interested in food, and reaching for the meal on your plate. In this chapter you'll see how to prep single-ingredient fruits, vegetables, and proteins for easy grasping and eating. Simple recipes introduce superfoods like kale, salmon, and berries.

This chapter includes a few purées as well. Feed your baby with a spoon (but pay attention to her cues) or make the purées thicker and allow her to self-feed, one handful at a time. Either way, follow your baby's lead. She's ready to start her eating adventure.

AT THIS STAGE

- Much of eating at this early stage is about your baby exploring—touching, smelling, and, yes, tasting. But don't be alarmed if it seems like little of the food is actually making it into her tummy. Self-feeding takes a lot of eye-hand coordination, and that's an ability your baby is still developing. If she seems particularly frustrated, consider spoon-feeding her a purée or mash, but keep offering finger foods at mealtimes.

- When self-feeding, your baby will likely use her whole palm for picking up food, so cut foods into long, thin sticks or make sure softer foods are thick enough to pick up by the handful.

- Skip added salt and sugars in foods you prepare for your baby.

- The portion sizes in this chapter are quite small: just 2 to 4 tablespoons. Even so, these are just guidelines. Your baby may eat more or less. Let her decide.

- Offer your baby water in a sippy cup or, even better, a small open cup to drink with her meal.

- Your baby's facial expressions will likely be pure gold as she tries new foods. Sometimes she will smile with delight; other times she will grimace or go wide-eyed with surprise. Even if your baby seems not to like a new food, don't take it away immediately. She may move back to it and try again. And remember, if she doesn't like a food, try it again in a week, then in a month, and then in another month in another form. In other words, don't give up! It can take a dozen (or more) tries for a baby to develop a taste for particular foods.

FOOD SAFETY BASICS

- Always wash your hands before cooking and after handling raw meat, poultry, or eggs.

- Wash thoroughly any cutting boards or utensils that have been in contact with raw meat, poultry, or eggs.

- Don't defrost foods on the countertop. Instead, thaw them in the fridge overnight or in the microwave. An overnight defrost usually yields the best results.

REMEMBER THE RULE OF THREES. MOST FOODS KEEP WELL IN THE FRIDGE FOR UP TO THREE DAYS AND IN THE FREEZER FOR UP TO THREE MONTHS.

- Food can stay at room temperature for up to two hours. Any longer than that and it needs to go in the refrigerator or freezer.

- Most foods (except for seafood, which can turn more quickly) keep well in the refrigerator for at least three days or in the freezer for up to three months.

SINGLE-INGREDIENT FINGER FOODS FOR BEGINNING EATERS

(ages 6 months and up)

★ **Benchmark size:** Length and width of adult pinky

★ **Benchmark softness:** Adult can easily mash with thumb and forefinger

STEAMED OR ROASTED CARROT

RIPE MANGO

CUCUMBER

STEAMED OR ROASTED BROCCOLI

PEELED AND STEAMED OR ROASTED SWEET POTATO

COOKED CHICKEN

RIPE PEACH SLICE

STEAMED GREEN BEANS

TOAST

COOKED PENNE PASTA

WATERMELON

CHEESE

HARD-BOILED EGG

PEELED AND STEAMED APPLE

BANANA

COOKED FISH, FLAKED

AVOCADO

PEELED AND
STEAMED PEAR

STEAMED OR ROASTED
ASPARAGUS

STEAMED OR ROASTED
ZUCCHINI SPEAR

STEAMED OR ROASTED
CAULIFLOWER

HOW TO STEAM

Steamed fruits and vegetables are ideal finger foods for beginning eaters. Your goal is a texture that is soft, but not so soft that the food disintegrates when your baby picks it up. A good rule of thumb: It should take just gentle pressure for you to mash the food with your fingers.

To steam fruits and veggies, cut the pieces into roughly the same size—think the width and length of your pinky finger. This will help each piece cook at an equal rate. Place a steamer basket over 1 inch of water in a medium saucepan. Bring the water to a boil. Add the food, cover, and cook until tender. Don't be shy about checking frequently for doneness. Remove the food from the pot with tongs and let cool before serving or storing.

Fruits and Veggies Ideal for Steaming

- Peeled apple slices
- Peeled pear slices
- Broccoli florets
- Cauliflower florets
- Carrot sticks
- Green beans
- Peeled potato sticks
- Peeled sweet potato sticks
- Zucchini sticks

Gagging versus Choking

"But won't she choke?" That's the reaction many people have when they hear about baby-led feeding for the first time.

Starting solids—especially finger foods—can be stressful for parents due to an intense fear of choking. Indeed, transitioning from a 100% liquid diet to solid food is a big developmental step for babies. They need to master many important skills and develop muscle strength before they can successfully manipulate solid food in their mouths.

Luckily, nature equipped babies with a perfect instrument to stay safe during this learning process: the gag reflex. Gagging is a natural process that allows babies to expel the food they are not yet equipped to swallow. As babies mature, their gagging reflex shifts closer to the back of the tongue and gagging occurs less frequently, and then finally at the same level as in adults at around age eight to nine months.

Although some amount of gagging occurs in almost all babies when solids are first started, excessive gagging may signal that your baby isn't quite ready for certain textures. If your baby gags frequently when served finger foods, it may make sense to step back and wait another week or two before continuing with solids. Or consider serving purées for a bit longer before trying again.

Gagging may also be a sign of oral motor delays or extreme sensitivities to the smell, texture, or flavor of food. Excessive gagging is not only very scary for parents—it is very unpleasant for babies, who may start associating mealtimes with discomfort. If your baby is very distressed by gagging or it occurs frequently and is accompanied by vomiting, talk to your doctor about a referral to a speech language pathologist or occupational therapist for an evaluation.

Choking, unlike gagging, can be life-threatening and should be avoided at all costs. Choking is more common in young children than in adults because children are just learning how to chew and their throats are smaller and more easily blocked by pieces of food.

HERE'S HOW TO STAY SAFE WHEN STARTING SOLIDS

KNOW THE DIFFERENCE BETWEEN CHOKING AND GAGGING

While gagging is often accompanied by a coughing or retching sound, choking is almost always silent. A choking baby may only cough or cry weakly. Some signs of choking include flapping or waving hands, staring with an open mouth, clutching the throat, and lips and under-eye areas turning blue.

PREVENT CHOKING BY CHOOSING SAFE FOODS

There is not a lot of good-quality research on the dangers of choking when feeding finger foods to babies. But researchers behind a recent randomized trial concluded that babies who are fed finger foods are not more likely to choke than those fed purées. To minimize choking, it is important to remember that any hard food that can snap off easily, such as hard raw vegetables and fruit, is not a good option for beginning eaters. To make hard foods a safe choice for your baby, cut them into matchstick shapes and cook slightly to soften.

BE GUIDED BY YOUR BABY'S READINESS

Babies who are not developmentally prepared for solids may continuously gag or choke even on thin purées. The thrust tongue reflex—where babies automatically push food out of their mouths with their tongues—that diminishes at around four months is, in fact, another safety system that protects babies from choking on solids. Both the thrust reflex and excessive gagging may be signs that your child needs more time before he can safely enjoy solid foods.

BE PREPARED

Learn infant and child first aid and CPR in a certified training course.

WATCH YOUR BABY AT ALL TIMES WHILE SHE'S EATING

Period. This is the most important prevention strategy parents can use.

ROASTED APPLE SLICES

To make apples tender enough for beginning eaters, you can steam them or, my favorite method, roast them. Cooked slowly in the oven, the fruit's flavors become even more concentrated and the apples take on an irresistible velvety texture.

1 APPLE, SUCH AS GALA, PEELED, HALVED, CORED, AND CUT INTO 8 WEDGES

1 TEASPOON OLIVE OIL

⅛ TEASPOON GROUND CARDAMOM (OPTIONAL)

⅛ TEASPOON GROUND CINNAMON (OPTIONAL)

1 Preheat the oven to 350°F. Line a baking sheet with parchment paper.

2 Place the apple slices on the prepared pan. Toss with the olive oil, and sprinkle with cardamom and cinnamon (if using).

3 Bake until tender, 25 to 30 minutes.

4 Cool and serve whole or cut into small pieces for more advanced eaters.

Makes 4 servings

MAKE AHEAD: Refrigerate for up to 3 days.

Nutrition per serving: 34 calories; 0g protein; 1g fat (0g sat. fat); 6g carbohydrates; 1g fiber; 5g sugars; 1mg sodium; 3mg calcium; 0.1mg iron; 49mg potassium; 2mg vitamin C; 25IU vitamin A

I like the idea of all this, but it feels like I'm constantly cleaning my kitchen. **Is there any way to minimize the mess?**

If you've spent any time on the Facebook baby-led weaning pages, you know that this feeding approach is capital-M *Messy*. Of course! BLF babies are exploring all sorts of foods, and this exploration can include smearing avocado on their ears and chewed-up sweet potato on the high chair or floor. Here are a few tips for handling the mess:

- Let your baby eat wearing only a diaper and a bib. After the meal? Bath time!

- Buy a bib with long arms and a pocket to catch food spills.

- Skip serving food in bowls or on plates. Just put it on a clean tray, since bowls or plates are likely to end up on the floor.

- Make sure your high chair is easy to clean, with a removable tray and easy-wipe seat.

- Place a drop cloth, large trash bag, or "splat mat" under your baby's high chair to protect the floor from spills.

- Invest in a small handheld vacuum and store it nearby.

- Consider getting a dog if you don't already have one. (Just kidding!) (Sort of.)

In the end, you have to embrace the mess. Your baby will become a neat eater as he gets older, and for now he's learning how to be a good eater, and that's even better.

BROCCOLI BROOMS

This vibrant green veg is easy and delicious served plain. But you can up the nutritional ante with the healthy fats in olive oil and the B vitamins in nutritional yeast. To get a head start on this recipe, wash, trim, and store the broccoli in a zip-top bag in the fridge up to 48 hours before steaming.

1 BUNCH BROCCOLI (ABOUT 1 POUND), CUT INTO FLORETS WITH 1 INCH OR SO OF STALK

2 TABLESPOONS NUTRITIONAL YEAST

2 TABLESPOONS OLIVE OIL

1 Place a steamer basket over 1 inch of water in a wide sauce-pan. Bring the water to a boil. Add the broccoli florets, cover, and steam until tender, 5 to 7 minutes. Cool.

2 Put the nutritional yeast in a small shallow dish. Quickly dip the head of each floret into a bit of olive oil and then sweep each floret in the nutritional yeast.

Makes about 8 servings

MAKE AHEAD: Plain steamed florets can be refrigerated for up to 3 days. Dip them in the olive oil and nutritional yeast just before serving.

Nutrition per serving: 54 calories; 2g protein; 4g fat (1g sat. fat); 4g carbohydrates; 2g fiber; 1g sugars; 19mg sodium; 27mg calcium; 0.5mg iron; 179mg potassium; 50mg vitamin C; 353IU vitamin A

SIMPLE POACHED SALMON

Serve fish early and often, especially omega-3 rich types like salmon, mackerel, and tuna (see page 148 for more information on tuna and mercury).

1 LEMON, HALVED

ONE 6-OUNCE FILLET SALMON, RINSED AND ANY BONES REMOVED

1 Choose a lidded pot in which your salmon fillet can lie flat. Fill the pot about halfway with water. Cut one half of the lemon into thin slices and add them to the water. Bring to a boil.

2 Reduce the heat to maintain a gentle simmer. Add the salmon. Cover the pot and cook for 5 minutes. Remove the pot from the heat and remove the lid. Let the salmon sit in the water for 10 minutes. Remove and discard the skin.

3 Cool to room temperature or serve chilled. Flake with a fork for easier grabbing and spritz with lemon juice from the remaining lemon half before serving.

Makes 6 servings

MAKE AHEAD: Refrigerate for up to 24 hours.

AGE IT UP: Poached salmon is delicious at any age. Serve it with lemony mayonnaise for dipping or flake it over pasta drizzled with olive oil and dressed with lemon.

Nutrition per serving: 46 calories; 6g protein; 2g fat (0.5g sat. fat); 0g carbohydrates; 0g fiber; 0g sugars; 13mg sodium; 4mg calcium; 0.1mg iron; 128mg potassium; 1mg vitamin C; 53IU vitamin A

Should you rinse fish and chicken?

Fish, maybe. Fish often needs a quick rinse since scales sometimes cling to the flesh. Chicken—no. Rinsing a whole chicken or chicken parts before cooking only encourages the spread of bacteria in the kitchen as potentially contaminated water splashes around your sink. Plus, any bacteria that could be dangerous to your family isn't going to simply wash down the drain. The chicken needs to be cooked thoroughly to kill the bacteria. In the end, rinsing chicken does some harm, potentially, and no good. Save a step and skip it.

ROASTED ZUCCHINI STICKS

Keeping the peel on the zucchini helps the roasted stick stay in one piece. Don't be surprised if your baby gums the softer part of the zucchini and leaves the peel behind. These super-simple veggie sticks are delicious on their own or dunked into marinara sauce.

1 ZUCCHINI

OLIVE OIL

ITALIAN-STYLE BREAD CRUMBS

1 Preheat the oven to 400°F. Line a baking sheet with parchment paper.

2 Cut the zucchini into sticks about 6 inches long and ¾ inch thick. Pour some olive oil onto a plate and spread some bread crumbs out in a shallow dish or pie plate.

3 Roll the sticks in the olive oil, then the bread crumbs. Place them on the prepared baking sheet.

4 Roast for 25 to 30 minutes, flipping once, or until the zucchini is tender and golden. Cool and serve.

Makes 4 servings

MAKE AHEAD: Refrigerate for up to 3 days. Re-crisp the bread crumbs by reheating the sticks in the oven for 5 minutes. Cool and serve.

Nutrition per serving: 98 calories; 1g protein; 7g fat (1g sat. fat); 8g carbohydrates; 1g fiber; 1g sugars; 20mg sodium; 8mg calcium; 0.3mg iron; 131mg potassium; 9mg vitamin C; 100IU vitamin A

OJ CHICKEN

Cooked covered in the oven, this chicken becomes almost unbelievably tender. Play with the flavors by substituting one lemon and one lime for the orange.

ZEST AND JUICE OF 1 LARGE NAVEL ORANGE

1 TABLESPOON OLIVE OIL

½ POUND CHICKEN TENDERS

1 Combine the orange zest, orange juice, and olive oil in a medium baking dish. Add the chicken tenders and marinate for at least 15 minutes and up to 2 hours. Cover and refrigerate if marinating for longer than 1 hour.

2 Preheat the oven to 350°F. Cover the baking dish with aluminum foil and bake for 35 to 40 minutes, or until the chicken is no longer pink when you cut into the fattest tender.

3 Discard the cooking liquid. Cool the chicken and shred or cut into chunks.

Makes 4 servings

MAKE AHEAD: Refrigerate for up to 3 days.

COOKING TIP: Be sure to wash citrus fruits before zesting.

Nutrition per serving: 178 calories; 7g protein; 11g fat (2g sat. fat); 12g carbohydrates; 1g fiber; 3g sugars; 226mg sodium; 10mg calcium; 0.6mg iron; 120mg potassium; 5mg vitamin C; 14IU vitamin A

BASIC BAKED OATMEAL

Oatmeal is one of those foods that seems perfect for babies, but it's not such a natural finger food. The solution? Bake, chill, and cut into sticks or cubes. For a more elaborate version, see page 122.

1 Preheat the oven to 400°F. Grease an 8 x 8 inch baking pan with butter.

2 In a large bowl, whisk together the oats and baking powder. Whisk in the melted butter, milk, and egg.

3 Pour the oat mixture into the prepared pan, making sure that the oats are spread out and submerged. Bake until no longer jiggly in the center, about 35 minutes.

4 Chill and cut into rectangles for serving.

Makes 12 servings

MAKE AHEAD: Refrigerate for up to 3 days.

1 TABLESPOON UNSALTED BUTTER, MELTED, PLUS MORE FOR THE PAN

2 CUPS ROLLED OATS

1 TEASPOON BAKING POWDER

2 CUPS WHOLE MILK

1 EGG

Nutrition per serving: 165 calories; 8g protein; 6g fat (2g sat. fat); 20g carbohydrates; 3g fiber; 2g sugars; 80mg sodium; 103mg calcium; 1.6mg iron; 203mg potassium; 1mg vitamin C; 196IU vitamin A

KALE and WHITE BEAN MASH

This purée is thick enough for your baby to simply scoop up with his hands or deliver to his mouth with a preloaded spoon. For a looser purée appropriate for spoon-feeding, thin the mixture with water, breastmilk, or formula.

1 TABLESPOON OLIVE OIL

1 GARLIC CLOVE, ROUGHLY CHOPPED

4 CUPS TORN LACINATO KALE LEAVES

ONE 15.5-OUNCE CAN LOW-SODIUM CANNELLINI BEANS, DRAINED AND RINSED

2 TEASPOONS FRESH LEMON JUICE

1 Heat the olive oil in a large skillet over medium heat. Add the garlic, reduce the heat to low, and cook for 2 minutes. Add the kale and cook, stirring, for 3 minutes. Remove from the heat and let cool for a few minutes.

2 Transfer the kale and garlic to a food processor. Pulse to finely chop the kale. Add the beans and lemon juice. Process until smooth.

3 Serve thick for hands-on eating or thin for parental spoon-feeding.

Makes about 1¼ cups

MAKE AHEAD: Refrigerate for up to 3 days.

MIX IT UP: To turn this purée into patties, form the mixture into 10 rounds about ½ inch thick and put them on a parchment-lined baking sheet. Drizzle with olive oil and bake in a preheated 350°F oven for 30 minutes. Let cool on the baking sheet. The patties will firm up as they cool.

WHOLESOME TIP: Lacinato kale is also known as Tuscan or dinosaur kale. It has flatter leaves than curly kale, and is more tender and less bitter.

Nutrition per serving (2 tablespoons): 48 calories; 2g protein; 2g fat (0g sat. fat); 7g carbohydrates; 2g fiber; 1g sugars; 70mg sodium; 37mg calcium; 0.5mg iron; 122mg potassium; 33mg vitamin C; 4,121IU vitamin A

EASY AVOCADO

Avocados, full of fiber and beneficial unsaturated fats, are an incredible first food for babies. Naturally soft, they are ideal blended into a smoothie, spread on toast, or even mashed and licked off a spoon. That said, they can be challenging finger foods—so darn slippery! Here's the trick:

Halve, pit, peel, and slice a ripe, but not mushy, avocado into 8 slices. Place panko bread crumbs, unsweetened shredded coconut, and/or ground flaxseeds on a small plate. Gently press the avocado into the mixture to adhere. The coating will give your baby something to hold on to, so the avocado actually makes it into her mouth, not just on the floor.

Nutrition per serving (¼ avocado with 2 teaspoons panko): 110 calories; 2g protein; 7g fat (1g sat. fat); 10g carbohydrates; 4g fiber; 0g sugars; 20mg sodium; 6mg calcium; 0.4mg iron; 244mg potassium; 5mg vitamin C; 73IU vitamin A

Nutrition per serving (¼ avocado with 2 teaspoons unsweetened coconut): 91 calories; 1g protein; 8g fat (2g sat. fat); 5g carbohydrates; 1g fiber; 1g sugars; 4mg sodium; 6mg calcium; 0.3mg iron; 253mg potassium; 5mg vitamin C; 73IU vitamin A

Nutrition per serving (¼ avocado with 2 teaspoons ground flaxseeds): 107 calories; 2g protein; 10g fat (1g sat. fat); 6g carbohydrates; 5g fiber; 0g sugars; 5mg sodium; 19mg calcium; 0.6mg iron; 284mg potassium; 5mg vitamin C; 73IU vitamin A

CINNAMON-BANANA PANCAKES

These sweet cakes contain no added sugar and no flour. Serve plain or spread with a thin layer of peanut butter or almond butter for an even more delicious snack or breakfast.

1 EGG

1 LARGE RIPE BANANA, MASHED (ABOUT ½ CUP)

⅛ TEASPOON GROUND CINNAMON

1 TABLESPOON UNSALTED BUTTER

1 Break the egg into a medium bowl and beat with a fork. Add the mashed banana and cinnamon and stir to combine. The batter will seem very runny.

2 Melt the butter on a large griddle or in a large, preferably nonstick, skillet. Drop the banana batter by tablespoonfuls onto the pan and cook until golden brown and cooked through, about 3 minutes on the first side and 1 to 2 minutes on the second. Cool and serve.

Makes 9 pancakes

MAKE AHEAD: Refrigerate for up to 3 days. Reheat briefly, or just serve cold or at room temperature.

Nutrition per serving (1 pancake): 30 calories; 1g protein; 2g fat (1g sat. fat); 3g carbohydrates; 0g fiber; 2g sugars; 7mg sodium; 4mg calcium; 0.1mg iron; 54mg potassium; 1mg vitamin C; 74IU vitamin A

EGGY TOFU

This recipe is an easy way to combine two power foods.

**ONE 14-OUNCE BLOCK
FIRM TOFU**

1 EGG

**1 TO 2 TABLESPOONS
OLIVE OIL**

1 Press the tofu to remove excess liquid: place the block on a plate lined with folded paper towels. Cover with more folded paper towels and set another plate on top. Place a heavy can (such as tomatoes) or a box of chicken broth on top. Let sit for 20 minutes. Remove the plate and paper towels.

2 Cut the tofu into 16 rectangles about 3 inches by 1 inch. Beat the egg in a shallow dish.

3 Heat the olive oil in a large, preferably nonstick, skillet over medium heat. Coat each piece of tofu in the egg, letting any excess drip off, and cook, working in batches if necessary, until golden brown, about 3 minutes per side. Add more olive oil to the pan between batches if needed. Cool and serve.

Makes 8 servings

MAKE AHEAD: Refrigerate for up to 2 days. Reheat briefly, or serve chilled or at room temperature.

Nutrition per serving: 58 calories; 5g protein; 4g fat (1g sat. fat); 1g carbohydrates; 1g fiber; 0g sugars; 14mg sodium; 103mg calcium; 1mg iron; 81mg potassium; 0mg vitamin C; 30IU vitamin A

BABY'S FIRST MEATBALLS

Once your baby has gotten the hang of eating these savory little nuggets, add finely chopped onion, garlic, and/or herbs to the meat before shaping.

1 Preheat the oven to 425°F. Line a baking sheet with aluminum foil and top with a wire rack.

2 Place the ground beef in a medium bowl and mix with a bit of pepper. Form into 10 elongated meatballs, more like cylinders, about 2 inches by 1 inch.

3 Transfer the meatballs to the rack. Bake until the center of each meatball registers 165°F on an instant-read thermometer, 20 to 25 minutes. Cool and serve.

Makes 10 meatballs

MAKE AHEAD: Refrigerate for up to 3 days. Reheat gently in the oven or the microwave.

AGE IT UP: Add ¾ teaspoon salt to the meat mixture with the pepper.

COOKING TIP: An instant-read thermometer belongs in everyone's kitchen arsenal. They're inexpensive and indispensable when it comes to roasting chicken or turkey or making meatballs or meat loaf.

1 POUND 85% LEAN GROUND BEEF

FRESHLY GROUND BLACK PEPPER

Nutrition per serving (1 meatball): 98 calories; 8g protein; 7g fat (3g sat. fat); 0g carbohydrates; 0g fiber; 0g sugars; 30mg sodium; 7mg calcium; 1mg iron; 134mg potassium; 0mg vitamin C; 0IU vitamin A

LAZY MOM'S BLACK BEANS

I suppose you could make the argument that opening a can of beans is the real lazy mom's way, and it's certainly a method I use often. But lately I have been taking advantage of the slow cooker to make these versatile, protein-rich foods. I like that there is no sodium added, unless I add it myself, and that I don't need to worry about BPA or any other chemicals in the cans. And unlike cooking dried beans on the stovetop, it's completely hands-off, and there's no need to soak the beans in advance.

1 Spray the insert of a large slow cooker with nonstick cooking spray. Add the beans and onion halves. Cover with 2 inches of water.

2 Cook on Low for 7 to 9 hours, or until the beans are tender. Discard the onion.

3 Serve the beans whole or mashed.

Makes 4½ cups beans

MAKE AHEAD: Be sure to store the beans in their cooking liquid. If you'd like to make a soup, keep all the cooking liquid; it makes for a flavorful broth. Beans will keep in the fridge for up to 5 days, and they freeze beautifully.

AGE IT UP: Season the beans with salt during cooking.

NONSTICK COOKING SPRAY

1 POUND DRIED BLACK BEANS, RINSED

1 WHITE ONION, HALVED

Nutrition per serving (2 tablespoons): 77 calories; 5g protein; 0g fat (0g sat. fat); 14g carbohydrates; 3g fiber; 1g sugars; 2mg sodium; 28mg calcium; 1.1mg iron; 336mg potassium; 0mg vitamin C; 0IU vitamin A

GARLICKY SPINACH

Garlic and lemon help greens sing. Plus, the vitamin C in the citrus makes the iron in the greens more bioavailable to your baby.

1 TABLESPOON OLIVE OIL

1 GARLIC CLOVE, FINELY CHOPPED

ONE 5-OUNCE PACKAGE BABY SPINACH

LEMON WEDGE

1 Heat the olive oil in a medium saucepan over medium heat. Add the garlic and cook until just fragrant, about 30 seconds.

2 Add the spinach and cook, stirring, until the spinach is wilted. Drain in a fine-mesh sieve, pushing out excess liquid.

3 Transfer the spinach to a cutting board and chop.

4 Spritz with lemon and let your baby feed herself by the handful.

Makes ½ cup (2 servings)

MAKE AHEAD: Refrigerate for up to 2 days.

Nutrition per serving (¼ cup): 79 calories; 2g protein; 7g fat (1g sat. fat); 3g carbohydrates; 2g fiber; 0g sugars; 55mg sodium; 70mg calcium; 2.3mg iron; 6mg potassium; 21mg vitamin C; 4,586IU vitamin A

MASHED POTATO

This recipe is for brave moms and dads who have the patience and good humor to cheer their baby on as he picks up mashed potatoes by the handful. It's a wonderful experience for your little one, since mashed potatoes are ideal for exploring. Just make sure to plan for bath time right after the meal! Once your baby has gotten the hang of these, add some flavorful mix-ins such as chopped chives, grated cheese, or turmeric.

1 Place the potato chunks in a medium saucepan. Add water to cover by 1 inch. Bring the water to a boil and cook until the potato is tender, about 15 minutes.

2 Drain the potato and return it to the pan. Place the pan over low heat and shake gently for about 30 seconds to dry out the potato chunks.

3 Transfer the potato to a medium bowl. Mash with a fork or potato masher. Mash in the butter until melted and incorporated. Cool to room temperature and serve.

Makes about 1 cup (4 servings)

MAKE AHEAD: Refrigerate for up to 2 days.

1 MEDIUM RUSSET POTATO, PEELED AND CHOPPED INTO ROUGHLY 1-INCH CHUNKS

2 TABLESPOONS UNSALTED BUTTER, AT ROOM TEMPERATURE

Nutrition per serving: 123 calories; 2g protein; 6g fat (4g sat. fat); 16g carbohydrates; 2g fiber; 1g sugars; 11mg sodium; 15mg calcium; 0.8mg iron; 413mg potassium; 6mg vitamin C; 185IU vitamin A

TOMATO CHICKEN

The tomatoes in this dish thicken as they cook, making an effortless sauce for the chicken.

1 TABLESPOON OLIVE OIL

1 LARGE CHICKEN BREAST (ABOUT ½ POUND)

1 CUP CRUSHED TOMATOES

1 Heat the olive oil in a medium skillet over medium-high heat. Add the chicken breast and cook until browned, about 4 minutes per side.

2 Add the tomatoes and bring to a simmer. Cover and cook, with the liquid just simmering, for about 12 minutes, or until the chicken is cooked through.

3 Cool, then shred the chicken using two forks or your fingers. Serve with the tomato sauce.

Makes 4 servings

MAKE AHEAD: Refrigerate for up to 3 days.

Nutrition per serving: 181 calories; 8g protein; 11g fat (2g sat. fat); 12g carbohydrates; 2g fiber; 3g sugars; 21mg sodium; 30mg calcium; 1.4mg iron; 284mg potassium; 6mg vitamin C; 423IU vitamin A

FIRST HUMMUS

Make this simple spread as smooth or lumpy as you like. Your baby will probably enjoy eating this squishy spread by the handful. Or serve it as a dip or spread on toast.

Place the chickpeas in a medium bowl and smash with a fork. Stir in the olive oil and lemon juice, continuing to smash.

Makes about 1 cup (8 servings)

MAKE AHEAD: Refrigerate for up to 3 days.

AGE IT UP: Season with salt and use as a dip or sandwich filling.

ONE 15-OUNCE CAN LOW-SODIUM CHICKPEAS, DRAINED AND RINSED

3 TABLESPOONS OLIVE OIL

1 TABLESPOON FRESH LEMON JUICE

Nutrition per serving (2 tablespoons): 108 calories; 3g protein; 6g fat (1g sat. fat); 12g carbohydrates; 2g fiber; 0g sugars; 120mg sodium; 17mg calcium; 0.8mg iron; 92mg potassium; 2mg vitamin C; 11IU vitamin A

LEMONY ROASTED FISH

There are so many things parents can do to start their babies off on the right foot nutritionally. Serving low-mercury fish early and often is near the top of the list.

ONE 6-OUNCE COD FILLET

1 TEASPOON OLIVE OIL

LEMON ZEST

LEMON WEDGE

1 Preheat the oven to 375°F. Line a baking sheet with parchment paper.

2 Place the fish on the prepared baking sheet. Rub with the olive oil and sprinkle with a pinch or two of lemon zest. Roast for 12 to 15 minutes, or just until the fish flakes easily when you insert a thin knife into the center. Spritz the fish with lemon juice. Cool and serve in large flakes.

Makes 4 servings

AGE IT UP: Roasting fish fillets is an easy way to get a healthy dinner on the table quickly, no matter what age your kids are. Just season both sides of the fish with salt and pepper before roasting.

Nutrition per serving: 45 calories; 8g protein; 1g fat (0g sat. fat); 0g carbohydrates; 0g fiber; 0g sugars; 23mg sodium; 7mg calcium; 0.2mg iron; 176mg potassium; 0mg vitamin C; 17IU vitamin A

CRINKLE-CUT CARROTS

Sure, you can steam baby carrots or carrot sticks. But veggies chopped with a crinkle cutter (available on Amazon.com and at kitchen supply stores) are easier for a baby to grasp, and they look cute, too.

3 CARROTS, PEELED

1 Place a steamer basket over 1 inch of water in a medium saucepan. Bring the water to a simmer.

2 Using a crinkle cutter, chop the carrots into sticks about 2½ inches long and ½ inch wide.

3 Put the carrot sticks in the steamer basket. Cover and steam until tender but not mushy, about 10 minutes.

4 Cool and serve plain or with a dip such as Roasted Zucchini and White Bean Dip (page 110).

Makes 6 servings

MAKE AHEAD: Refrigerate for up to 3 days. Serve chilled or at room temperature.

Nutrition per serving: 13 calories; 0g protein; 0g fat (0g sat. fat); 3g carbohydrates; 1g fiber; 1g sugars; 21mg sodium; 10mg calcium; 0.1mg iron; 98mg potassium; 2mg vitamin C; 5,095IU vitamin A

Spiced
CHICKEN *and* SWEET POTATO PURÉE

Babies who eat only finger foods can have a hard time getting adequate iron and zinc in their daily diets, especially babies who are breastfed (since formula is fortified). This purée provides both of those nutrients, plus a boatload of vitamin A, in a tasty package. If you have an immersion blender, this is the time to use it. Otherwise, a food processor or regular blender will do the trick.

1 TABLESPOON OLIVE OIL

¼ CUP FINELY CHOPPED ONION

¼ TEASPOON GROUND CUMIN

¼ TEASPOON GROUND CINNAMON

1 SWEET POTATO, PEELED AND CHOPPED INTO LARGE CUBES (ABOUT 1¼ CUPS)

1 BONELESS, SKINLESS CHICKEN BREAST (ABOUT 8 OZ.), CUT INTO 1½-INCH CHUNKS

1 Heat the olive oil in a large skillet. Add the onion, reduce the heat to low, and cook for 5 minutes, or until the onion is soft. Add the cumin and cinnamon and cook for another minute.

2 Add the sweet potato chunks. Cover with 1½ cups water. Bring to a boil, reduce the heat to maintain a simmer, cover, and cook for 5 minutes.

3 Add the chicken. Simmer, partially covered, for 10 minutes, or until the chicken is cooked through and the sweet potato is soft. Let cool for a few minutes.

4 For a smooth mash, transfer the contents of the skillet to a bowl and blend with an immersion blender. For a chunkier meal, use a knife and fork to cut the chicken and sweet potato into small pieces.

5 Cool and spoon-feed your baby. Or offer to your baby on a pre-loaded spoon or spread on toast sticks.

Makes 2 cups (8 servings)

MAKE AHEAD: Refrigerate for up to 3 days.

Nutrition per serving (¼ cup): 82 calories; 9g protein; 2g fat (0g sat. fat); 5g carbohydrates; 1g fiber; 1g sugars; 33mg sodium; 7mg calcium; 0.2mg iron; 77mg potassium; 1mg vitamin C; 2,948IU vitamin A

MINI TURKEY PATTIES

While you can certainly cook up just plain turkey burgers, woodsy sage and flavorful mustard make these protein-rich patties more interesting for your baby's developing palate.

1 In a large bowl, combine the ground turkey, sage, and mustard. Form into 12 small patties.

2 Heat the olive oil in a large skillet over medium-high heat. Add the turkey patties and cook until no longer pink in the center, 3 to 4 minutes per side. Take care not to crowd the patties in the skillet; cook in batches, if necessary. Cool and serve.

Makes 12 patties

MAKE AHEAD: Refrigerate for up to 3 days.

AGE IT UP: We love these little burgers as sliders in my family. I up the mustard to 1 tablespoon, add ¾ teaspoon salt, and season with freshly ground black pepper.

1 POUND GROUND TURKEY, PREFERABLY DARK MEAT

2 TABLESPOONS CHOPPED FRESH SAGE

2 TEASPOONS DIJON MUSTARD

2 TABLESPOONS OLIVE OIL

Nutrition per serving (1 patty): 89 calories; 6g protein; 7g fat (2g sat. fat); 0g carbohydrates; 0g fiber; 0g sugars; 40mg sodium; 12mg calcium; 0.5mg iron; 76mg potassium; 0mg vitamin C; 38IU vitamin A

GOLDEN EGGS WITH PEAS

Scrambled eggs are an ideal early food—completely soft and bursting with nutrition. They're perfect for busy parents, too, since they take less than five minutes to cook. Win-win!

1 EGG

⅛ TEASPOON GROUND TURMERIC

1 TEASPOON UNSALTED BUTTER

1 TABLESPOON FROZEN PEAS

1 Crack the egg into a small bowl. Add the turmeric and stir to combine with a fork.

2 Melt the butter in a small nonstick skillet over medium heat. Add the peas and cook, stirring frequently, until they are mostly defrosted, 1 to 2 minutes.

3 Add the egg and stir gently with a rubber spatula until large curds form and the egg is no longer runny.

4 Cool, break into curds, and serve.

Makes 1 serving

Nutrition per serving: 105 calories; 6g protein; 8g fat (4g sat. fat); 1g carbohydrates; 0g fiber; 1g sugars; 71mg sodium; 27mg calcium; 0.9mg iron; 73mg potassium; 1mg vitamin C; 517IU vitamin A

ROSEMARY ROOTS

For obvious reasons—think bright red baby hands, face, and, ahem, diaper—I *highly* recommend using golden beets in this recipe. Covering the baking sheet with aluminum foil for the first 15 minutes of roasting helps ensure the vegetables become tender throughout.

3 GOLDEN BEETS, PEELED AND CUT INTO WEDGES

1 LARGE PARSNIP, PEELED AND CUT INTO STICKS, WOODY CORES REMOVED

1 LARGE CARROT, CUT INTO STICKS

1 TABLESPOON OLIVE OIL

2 TEASPOONS FINELY CHOPPED FRESH ROSEMARY

1 Preheat the oven to 425°F. Line a baking sheet with parchment paper.

2 Place the veggies on the prepared baking sheet. Toss with the olive oil and rosemary. Cover the pan tightly with aluminum foil and bake for 15 minutes.

3 Remove the foil and bake until tender and browned, 25 to 30 minutes more. Cool and serve.

Makes 8 servings

MAKE AHEAD: Refrigerate for up to 3 days.

AGE IT UP: This colorful recipe will be welcome throughout the years on your dinner table. For more flavor, season the veggies well with salt and pepper before roasting.

Nutrition per serving: 47 calories; 1g protein; 2g fat (0g sat. fat); 7g carbohydrates; 2g fiber; 3g sugars; 32mg sodium; 24mg calcium; 0.6mg iron; 199mg potassium; 5mg vitamin C; 1,540IU vitamin A

SESAME SOBA NOODLES

Babies plus noodles equals a match made in heaven.

1 Cook the soba noodles in boiling water according to the package directions. Drain, rinse with cold water, and pat dry with a paper towel. Transfer to a medium bowl.

2 Toss the noodles with the sesame oil and sesame seeds.

Makes about 1½ cups (4 servings)

MAKE AHEAD: Refrigerate for up to 3 days.

3 OUNCES SOBA NOODLES

1 TEASPOON TOASTED SESAME OIL (OR COCONUT OIL)

¼ TEASPOON SESAME SEEDS

Nutrition per serving: 83 calories; 3g protein; 1g fat (0g sat. fat); 16g carbohydrates; 0g fiber; 0g sugars; 168mg sodium; 10mg calcium; 0.6mg iron; 55mg potassium; 0mg vitamin C; 0IU vitamin A

STRAWBERRY AND GOAT CHEESE SPREAD

I prefer starting with frozen strawberries here since their natural juices help make this tangy spread smooth and creamy—not to mention a pretty pink.

1 CUP FROZEN STRAWBERRIES

2 OUNCES FRESH GOAT CHEESE (CHÈVRE)

1 Put the strawberries in a microwave-safe bowl and defrost in the microwave for 1 minute. (Or defrost in the fridge overnight.)

2 Place the goat cheese in a medium bowl. Add the strawberries and mash with a fork. Stir to combine.

3 To serve, spread thinly on toast, use as a dip, or let your baby eat it with a spoon (yum).

Makes about 1 cup

MAKE AHEAD: Refrigerate for up to 2 days.

Nutrition per serving (2 tablespoons): 25 calories; 1g protein; 2g fat (1g sat. fat); 2g carbohydrates; 0g fiber; 1g sugars; 26mg sodium; 13mg calcium; 0.2mg iron; 31mg potassium; 11mg vitamin C; 75IU vitamin A

AVOCADO-BEET DIP

I often save cooking time by buying the precooked, vacuum-packed beets I find in my grocery store's produce section. Look for brands like Love or Melissa's. Or, peel and steam fresh beets, following the instructions on page 43. This dip is super-creamy and just a bit earthy.

Coarsely chop the avocado and beets. Put them in a food processor, add the lime juice and process until smooth. Serve with steamed vegetables for dipping or as a spread on toast or crackers.

Makes ¾ cup (6 servings)

MAKE AHEAD: Refrigerate for up to 1 day.

1 RIPE AVOCADO, HALVED, PITTED, AND PEELED

4 OUNCES COOKED BEETS (2 SMALL)

1 TEASPOON FRESH LIME JUICE

Nutrition per serving (2 tablespoons): 62 calories; 1g protein; 5g fat (1g sat. fat); 5g carbohydrates; 3g fiber; 2g sugars; 17mg sodium; 7mg calcium; 0.3mg iron; 221mg potassium; 4mg vitamin C; 56IU vitamin A

TEFF PORRIDGE

Teff is an ancient grain that's a staple of Ethiopian diets and a nutritional superstar. Find it online or in health food stores from brands such as Bob's Red Mill. I've fallen in love with its nutty taste, and I think you and your baby will, too.

½ CUP TEFF (NOT TEFF FLOUR)

1½ CUPS WATER

UNSALTED BUTTER, FOR SERVING

1 In a small saucepan, toast the teff over medium heat, stirring frequently, until fragrant, 3 to 5 minutes. Remove the pot from the heat and carefully add the water (it may spatter).

2 Bring the water to a boil, cover, and simmer, stirring occasionally, until the teff is thick and creamy, about 15 minutes.

3 Top each serving with a pat of butter, cool, and serve. Let your baby eat with a preloaded spoon or his hands (such fun!). To thin the porridge for parental spoon-feeding, stir in breastmilk or formula.

Makes 1½ cups (6 servings)

VARIATION: For teff "fingers," transfer the cooked teff to a buttered loaf pan. Cool, cover, and refrigerate until firm. Cut into rectangles.

MAKE AHEAD: Refrigerate for up to 3 days. Reheat gently, adding a little water, breastmilk, or formula if desired for a smoother texture.

Nutrition per serving (¼ cup), without butter: 59 calories; 2g protein; 0g fat (0g sat. fat); 13g carbohydrates; 1g fiber; 0g sugars; 2mg sodium; 29mg calcium; 1.2mg iron; 69mg potassium; 0mg vitamin C; 1IU vitamin A

TOASTS OF THE TOWN

Toast is an excellent early finger food. Cut into strips, it's easy for babies to grasp and a perfect vehicle for various spreads. These spreads serve a few purposes: exposing your baby to common allergens (with an aim toward preventing them; see page 18), introducing new flavors, and providing nutrition. Don't be alarmed if your baby spends more time licking and sucking on the spread than actually eating the bread. He's exploring taste and texture, and will start nibbling away on the toast before you know it. Start with a thin layer of spread, especially of sticky nut butters—thick globs of nut butters can be a choking hazard.

Super Spreads

- Peanut butter
- Almond butter
- Sunflower butter
- Jam
- Tahini
- Cream cheese
- Unsalted butter
- Pesto
- Hummus
- Mashed banana
- Mashed avocado

BUY THE BEST BREAD

With so many loaves of bread on the supermarket shelf, it can be hard to know which to choose. First step, check out the ingredient list and make sure the word "whole" is included in the first ingredient. "Wheat flour" is not the same as "whole-wheat flour." Babies do not need to eat whole-wheat all the time since their tummies may be too small for lots of fiber, but if you serve whole wheat about half the time, it will give them a chance to get used to the texture. Next, make sure there are at least 2 grams of fiber per slice and no more than 2 grams of sugar (preferably less).

chapter
three

HEARTIER
FINGER FOODS

(8 months and up)

As your baby becomes a more confident self-feeder—and develops a few teeth—eating is only going to get more fun. Between the ages of eight and ten months, most babies master a pincer grasp, enabling them to pick up smaller pieces of food. So while you can continue with wedge-shaped finger foods, start cutting most of the food you offer into small pieces so your baby can practice her handy new self-feeding method. A good general guideline is to think of chickpea-size pieces, and continue to avoid hard foods like whole nuts and candy.

Around this age, start transitioning your baby to a cup with a straw, or introduce an open cup. This will help her develop a new set of muscles and improve her drinking skills.

At around 10 months, your baby will also become more coordinated with a spoon, so continue to serve thick soups or mashes that she can spoon-feed herself, drink from the bowl, or simply pick up with her hands in the case of heartier purées.

If you have been supplementing finger foods with parental spoon-feeding, consider phasing the practice out around this stage, or whenever your baby is a capable and confident self-feeder. Many babies reject spoon-feeding at about this age as their desire for autonomy and self-feeding increases. It's a big step in their lifelong eating adventure.

COOKED CORN

STEAMED EDAMAME

CHEESE

FIGS

STEAMED APPLE

STEAMED ASPARAGUS

STEAMED POTATO

RIPE PEACH

SMASHED BLUEBERRIES

RIPE MANGO

CHOPPED RASPBERRIES

COOKED PEAS

COOKED SMALL
PASTA

HARD-BOILED EGG

STEAMED SWEET POTATO

STEAMED CARROTS   CHOPPED STRAWBERRIES   CHOPPED BANANA   RIPE MELON   STEAMED CAULIFLOWER

CHOPPED GRAPES   STEAMED BUTTERNUT SQUASH   OMELET   SMASHED CHICKPEAS   RIPE PAPAYA

SINGLE-INGREDIENT FINGER FOODS FOR MORE ADVANCED EATERS

(ages 8 months and up)

★ **Benchmark size:** Chickpea, although there are exceptions, such as broccoli florets

★ **Benchmark softness:** Adult can mash with thumb and forefinger

BROCCOLI and HAM EGG MUFFINS ❄

These savory little bites have a lot going for them. They're ideal any time of day—breakfast, lunch, snack, or dinner. They're portable: Tote them to daycare or just out and about. And they are also easily customizable. Instead of broccoli and ham finely chop 1¼ cups cooked veggies and/or meat to use up what's in your fridge. If your mini-muffin cups are on the larger side, this will make 12 muffins; if the cups are smaller, you may be able to make more.

NONSTICK COOKING SPRAY

1 CUP VERY FINELY CHOPPED COOKED BROCCOLI

1 SLICE HAM, VERY FINELY CHOPPED (ABOUT ¼ CUP)

4 EGGS

FRESHLY GROUND BLACK PEPPER

1 Preheat the oven to 350°F. Spray 12 mini-muffin cups with nonstick cooking spray.

2 Stir together the broccoli and ham. Divide evenly among the muffin cups.

3 In a medium measuring cup, whisk together the eggs and pepper to taste. Pour the eggs over the broccoli mixture in the muffin cups, dividing them evenly.

4 Bake for 25 minutes, or until set. Cool in the muffin cups for 10 minutes. Transfer to a wire rack to cool. Serve warm or at room temperature.

Makes 12 mini muffins

MAKE AHEAD: Refrigerate for up to 3 days. Serve cold, at room temperature, or briefly reheated.

Nutrition per serving (1 muffin): 123 calories; 11g protein; 8g fat (3g sat. fat); 1g carbohydrates; 0g fiber; 0g sugars; 149mg sodium; 53mg calcium; 1.6mg iron; 147mg potassium; 7mg vitamin C; 572IU vitamin A

COOKING TIP

Mini-muffin tins make for perfectly portioned nibbles for baby. But if you only have standard-size muffin cups, that's okay, too—just increase the cooking time for any muffin recipe in this book. Check in 5-minute intervals for doneness, and make a note of how long the baking took for next time you prepare the recipe.

SWEET POTATO HUMMUS

Canned sweet potatoes will work fine here (just make sure there are no other ingredients in the can). Or simply roast a whole sweet potato in a 425°F oven until tender and let it cool. I sometimes roast several sweet potatoes at once, store some in the fridge, and then freeze the flesh of others for when I'm craving this sweet-and-smoky dip. Serve it with steamed or roasted vegetables for dipping, spread on toast, or offer to your baby on a preloaded spoon.

ONE 15-OUNCE CAN LOW-SODIUM CHICKPEAS, DRAINED AND RINSED

¾ CUP MASHED SWEET POTATOES

¼ CUP TAHINI (SESAME SEED PASTE)

½ TEASPOON GROUND CUMIN

1 TO 3 TABLESPOONS WATER

Place the chickpeas, sweet potatoes, tahini, cumin, and 1 tablespoon of the water in a food processor. Process until very smooth, 2 to 3 minutes, adding the remaining water 1 tablespoon at a time if you prefer a thinner consistency.

Makes about 2¼ cups

MAKE AHEAD: Refrigerate for up to 3 days.

AGE IT UP: Add ¾ teaspoon salt when processing.

Nutrition per serving (2 tablespoons): 60 calories; 2g protein; 2g fat (0g sat. fat); 8g carbohydrates; 2g fiber; 0g sugars; 87mg sodium; 26mg calcium; 1mg iron; 77mg potassium; 2mg vitamin C; 912IU vitamin A

Help! My mother (or mother-in-law or babysitter or daycare provider) thinks I'm crazy for practicing baby-led feeding. What should I say to her?

For those unfamiliar with baby-led feeding, giving finger foods to babies who are just starting solids may seem unusual, or even dangerous. Explain to your mother that baby-led feeding is becoming an ever more popular choice, since it promotes the eating of fresh, healthy whole foods and encourages a baby's exploration and independence. You may want to add that your pediatrician is in the loop and approves of your choice. Emphasize to anyone who cares for your child that your baby must be closely supervised when she eats; just because she's feeding herself doesn't mean she can be left unattended. You can find a Baby-Led Feeding Cheat Sheet to photocopy or print out for daycare providers, babysitters, or even grandparents on page 208 and at jennahelwig.com/blog/blf-cheatsheet.

Pumpkin
FRENCH TOAST STICKS

This is an easy recipe to double, triple, or even quadruple, as your family grows and gets hungrier. Older kids (and grownups) will enjoy these with a drizzle of maple syrup.

1 EGG

¼ CUP WHOLE MILK

¼ CUP CANNED PURE PUMPKIN PURÉE

PINCH OF GROUND NUTMEG

PINCH OF GROUND CINNAMON

PINCH OF GROUND CLOVES

1 TABLESPOON UNSALTED BUTTER

2 SLICES WHOLE-WHEAT SANDWICH BREAD, CUT INTO 8 STICKS

1 In a shallow dish, beat together the egg, milk, pumpkin purée, nutmeg, cinnamon, and cloves with a fork.

2 Melt the butter in a large skillet or on a griddle over medium heat. Dip the bread sticks into the pumpkin mixture, letting the bread soak up a little liquid and making sure all the bread is wet. Cook the French toast sticks in the butter until golden brown all over, about 3 minutes per side. Cool and serve.

Makes 4 servings

MAKE AHEAD: Refrigerate for up to 3 days. Serve cold, at room temperature, or briefly reheated.

COOKING TIP: Avoid crowding the pan when you're cooking, or the food will steam instead of brown. Cook the French toast sticks in batches if your pan is small, adding more butter if necessary.

Nutrition per serving: 120 calories; 4g protein; 6g fat (3g sat. fat); 14g carbohydrates; 2g fiber; 2g sugars; 103mg sodium; 37mg calcium; 1.1mg iron; 143mg potassium; 1mg vitamin C; 2,553IU vitamin A

MIX-AND-MATCH OMELETS

Protein-rich eggs are often a hit with babies, and these quick-prep omelets are a smart vehicle to introduce a variety of vegetables. Feel free to combine more than one add-in; just make sure they equal about a tablespoon.

1 Heat the olive oil or butter in a 5-inch nonstick pan over medium heat. Stir in any add-ins, except for any cheese (if using).

2 Add the egg. As it cooks, use a rubber spatula to lift up the sides of the omelet, allowing uncooked egg to come into contact with the bottom of the pan. After about a minute, when just a little runny on top, flip the omelet and cook for another 30 seconds. Sprinkle with cheese (if using). Transfer to a plate, cool, and cut into squares.

Makes 1 serving

EQUIPMENT TIP: I rarely recommend buying a specific piece of cooking equipment for just one use. But an inexpensive 5-inch nonstick pan is so perfect for making one-egg omelets that I think it's worth it. An 8-inch pan works, too, but you'll end up with a thinner omelet.

1 TEASPOON OLIVE OIL OR UNSALTED BUTTER

1 TABLESPOON FINELY CHOPPED ADD-INS (OPTIONAL)

1 EGG, BEATEN

ADD-IN IDEAS

- Cooked broccoli
- Cooked cauliflower
- Cooked asparagus
- Cooked mushrooms
- Fresh herbs
- Smoked salmon
- Ham
- Tomatoes
- Avocado
- Shredded cheese

Nutrition per omelet (without add-ins): 99 calories; 6g protein; 8g fat (4g sat. fat); 0g carbohydrates; 0g fiber; 0g sugars; 63mg sodium; 26mg calcium; 0.8mg iron; 62mg potassium; 0mg vitamin C; 363IU vitamin A

Peanut Butter

MINI MUFFIN BITES

These petite muffins were inspired by a recipe on Sally Kuzemchak's wonderful blog *Real Mom Nutrition*, and they make for a quick breakfast or satisfying snack. Serve plain or with a smear of butter.

NONSTICK COOKING SPRAY

½ CUP PITTED AND CHOPPED DATES

¼ CUP HOT WATER

½ CUP WHOLE MILK

¼ CUP PEANUT BUTTER

1 EGG

1½ CUPS ROLLED OATS

1 TEASPOON BAKING POWDER

1 TEASPOON GROUND CINNAMON

1 Preheat the oven to 375°F. Spray a 24-cup mini-muffin tin with nonstick cooking spray.

2 Place the dates in a small bowl. Add the hot water and mash with a fork so the dates are mostly a paste. It's okay if they're still a little lumpy.

3 In a large bowl, stir together the date mixture, milk, peanut butter, and egg. Add the oats, baking powder, and cinnamon. Stir to combine.

4 Divide the batter among the prepared muffin cups. Bake for 12 to 15 minutes, until the muffins are lightly browned and spring back when you push gently. Cool for 10 minutes in the pan and then transfer to a wire rack to cool completely.

Makes 24 mini muffins

MAKE AHEAD: Store in an airtight container at room temperature for up to 3 days.

AGE IT UP: Add ¼ teaspoon salt to the batter before baking.

Nutrition per serving (1 muffin): 67 calories; 3g protein; 2g fat (1g sat. fat); 10g carbohydrates; 2g fiber; 2g sugars; 22mg sodium; 31mg calcium; 0.6mg iron; 74mg potassium; 0mg vitamin C; 21IU vitamin A

MISO TOFU STICKS

Tofu and other less-processed soy foods like edamame and tempeh are smart additions to your baby's diet, whether or not your family is vegetarian. Contrary to some online chatter, eating soy does not increase the level of estrogens in humans, so don't have any qualms about preparing this superfood for your baby.

1 Preheat the oven to 400°F. Line a baking sheet with parchment paper.

2 To press the tofu, place the tofu block on a plate lined with a few folded paper towels. Cover the tofu with more paper towels. Place another plate on top and weigh it down with something heavy like a box of chicken broth or a can of tomatoes. Let the tofu drain for 20 minutes.

3 In a small bowl, whisk together the miso, vinegar, and sesame oil.

4 Remove the plate and paper towels and cut the tofu into 8 sticks. Coat each piece of tofu with the miso mixture and place on the prepared baking sheet. Sprinkle with the sesame seeds.

5 Bake for 25 to 30 minutes, or until the miso mixture is dry and browned.

6 Cool and serve in sticks or cut into cubes for more advanced eaters who can pick up smaller pieces of food.

Makes 8 servings

MAKE AHEAD: Refrigerate for up to 3 days.

Nutrition per serving: 60 calories; 5g protein; 4g fat (1g sat. fat); 2g carbohydrates; 1g fiber; 1g sugars; 73mg sodium; 117mg calcium; 1mg iron; 85mg potassium; 0mg vitamin C; 0IU vitamin A

ONE 14- TO 16-OUNCE PACKAGE EXTRA-FIRM TOFU

2 TABLESPOONS WHITE MISO

1 TABLESPOON RICE VINEGAR

1 TABLESPOON TOASTED SESAME OIL

½ TEASPOON WHITE OR BLACK SESAME SEEDS

Whole-Grain

ZUCCHINI BANANA BREAD

This easy recipe marries two quick bread classics. Your baby—and you—will devour it. Spelt is a nutty, not-too-dense whole-grain flour that's available in more and more grocery stores and natural food markets these days. If you can't find it, sub in whole-wheat pastry flour.

NONSTICK COOKING SPRAY

2 EGGS

½ CUP SUGAR

⅓ CUP CANOLA OIL

3 RIPE BANANAS, MASHED (ABOUT 1½ CUPS)

1 TABLESPOON VANILLA EXTRACT

1 CUP ALL-PURPOSE FLOUR

1 CUP SPELT OR WHOLE-WHEAT PASTRY FLOUR

1½ TEASPOONS GROUND CINNAMON

1 TEASPOON BAKING SODA

2 CUPS GRATED ZUCCHINI

1 Preheat the oven to 350°F. Spray a 9 x 5-inch loaf pan with nonstick cooking spray.

2 In a large bowl, whisk together the eggs, sugar, canola oil, mashed bananas, and vanilla. Add the flours, cinnamon, and baking soda and stir until almost combined. Add the zucchini and stir to combine.

3 Pour the batter into the prepared loaf pan. Bake for 55 to 60 minutes, or until the top is golden brown and a toothpick inserted into the center of the loaf comes out clean. Cool in the pan on a wire rack for 15 minutes, then remove from the pan and cool completely on the rack.

4 Slice, then cut the slices into small pieces and serve.

Makes 1 loaf (12 servings)

MAKE AHEAD: Store well-wrapped at room temperature for up to 3 days.

AGE IT UP: Add ¾ teaspoon salt to the batter for best flavor.

Nutrition per serving: 202 calories; 4g protein; 7g fat (1g sat. fat); 32g carbohydrates; 3g fiber; 13g sugars; 13mg sodium; 17mg calcium; 0.8mg iron; 220mg potassium; 6mg vitamin C; 102IU vitamin A

Raspberry-Rye
PANCAKES

These tender cakes make for a substantial breakfast or snack for little ones. Rye flour adds whole-grain goodness.

1 Place the raspberries in a bowl and let sit at room temperature while you mix together the pancake batter.

2 In a large bowl, whisk together the egg, milk, yogurt, and vanilla. Add the flours, baking powder, cinnamon, and baking soda. Stir to combine. Let rest for 5 minutes, then stir in the raspberries and any juices that have collected in the bowl.

3 Heat a griddle or skillet over medium heat. Grease with canola oil. Working in batches so as not to crowd the pan, drop 2-tablespoon rounds of the batter into the pan. Cook until golden brown and cooked through, 3 to 4 minutes per side.

Makes about 14 pancakes

MAKE AHEAD: Refrigerate for up to 3 days.

AGE IT UP: Add a couple of pinches of salt and 1 tablespoon sugar to the batter. Serve with maple syrup.

1 CUP FROZEN RASPBERRIES

1 EGG

½ CUP WHOLE MILK

½ CUP PLAIN FULL-FAT GREEK YOGURT

1 TEASPOON VANILLA EXTRACT

½ CUP ALL-PURPOSE FLOUR

½ CUP RYE FLOUR OR WHOLE-WHEAT PASTRY FLOUR

¾ TEASPOON BAKING POWDER

½ TEASPOON GROUND CINNAMON

¼ TEASPOON BAKING SODA

CANOLA OIL, FOR GREASING THE PAN

Nutrition per serving (1 pancake): 61 calories; 3g protein; 2g fat (1g sat. fat); 9g carbohydrates; 1g fiber; 1g sugars; 16mg sodium; 35mg calcium; 0.5mg iron; 77mg potassium; 3mg vitamin C; 41IU vitamin A

CURRIED CAULIFLOWER

Coating cauliflower in yogurt and spices gives it a savory, golden crust that makes this vegetable irresistible.

½ CUP PLAIN FULL-FAT GREEK YOGURT

3 TABLESPOONS CHOPPED FRESH CHIVES OR SCALLION GREENS

2 TABLESPOONS OLIVE OIL

2 TEASPOONS CURRY POWDER

1 TEASPOON GROUND TURMERIC

FRESHLY GROUND BLACK PEPPER

1 MEDIUM HEAD CAULIFLOWER, BROKEN INTO SMALL FLORETS (ABOUT 8 CUPS)

1 Preheat the oven to 425°F. Line a baking sheet with parchment paper.

2 In a large bowl, combine the yogurt, chives, olive oil, curry powder, turmeric, and pepper to taste. Add the cauliflower florets and toss so the cauliflower is thoroughly coated.

3 Transfer the cauliflower to the prepared baking sheet. Roast until tender and well browned, 45 to 50 minutes. Cool and serve.

Makes 6 servings

MAKE AHEAD: Refrigerate for up to 3 days.

AGE IT UP: Let this dish grace your table for years to come. Add ¾ teaspoon salt to the yogurt mixture, and then sprinkle the cooked cauliflower with another ¼ teaspoon salt before serving.

DAIRY RULES: Babies under the age of one should drink breast-milk or formula, not cow's milk. But it's fine—great!—to serve your baby yogurt and cheese made with cow's milk, or to use milk in baked goods or cooking from time to time. Just make sure to use full-fat dairy until age two.

Nutrition per serving: 93 calories; 4g protein; 7g fat (1g sat. fat); 6g carbohydrates; 3g fiber; 2g sugars; 35mg sodium, 38mg calcium; 0.9mg iron; 343mg potassium; 64mg vitamin C; 613IU vitamin A

ZUCCHINI *and* WHITE BEAN DIP

Roasted

Steamed carrot sticks, broccoli florets, and cauliflower make excellent dippers for this savory, fiber-filled dip. Or you can spread it on toast or serve on a preloaded spoon.

1 MEDIUM ZUCCHINI, COARSELY CHOPPED (ABOUT 2 CUPS)

3 TABLESPOONS OLIVE OIL

ONE 15-OUNCE CAN LOW-SODIUM CANNELLINI BEANS

2 TABLESPOONS GRATED PARMESAN CHEESE

1 GARLIC CLOVE, COARSELY CHOPPED

5 FRESH BASIL LEAVES

FRESHLY GROUND BLACK PEPPER

1 Preheat the oven to 425°F. Line a baking sheet with parchment paper.

2 Place the zucchini on the baking sheet and drizzle with 1 tablespoon of the olive oil. Toss with your hands to coat the zucchini. Roast until very tender, about 25 minutes. Cool for at least 10 minutes.

3 Transfer to a food processor and add the remaining 2 tablespoons olive oil, the beans, cheese, garlic, basil, and pepper to taste. Process until smooth, adding a tablespoon or two of water if you prefer a thinner dip.

Makes about 1¼ cups

MAKE AHEAD: Refrigerate for up to 3 days. To get a head start on the recipe, roast the zucchini up to 24 hours ahead and refrigerate until ready to use.

AGE IT UP: This dip would be right at home on a crudité platter or served with breadsticks. Add ½ teaspoon salt as you process, then taste for seasoning and add more salt, pepper, or Parmesan, if desired. Serve drizzled with a little more olive oil.

WHOLESOME TIP: If you can find it, opt for Parmigiano-Reggiano cheese imported from Italy. It is pricier than domestic Parmesan cheeses, but packs a load of flavor. Plus, some grated domestic brands are packaged with unappealing fillers.

Nutrition per serving (2 tablespoons): 75 calories; 2g protein; 4g fat (1g sat. fat); 7g carbohydrates; 2g fiber; 0g sugars; 104mg sodium; 14mg calcium; 0.1mg iron; 58mg potassium; 4mg vitamin C; 67IU vitamin A

SWEET POTATO NUGGETS

To get the mash, cook a sweet potato in the oven or microwave, or just use canned. If you opt for canned, you may need to stir in extra panko if the sweet potato mixture seems especially soft.

1 Preheat the oven to 400°F. Line a baking sheet with parchment paper.

2 In a medium bowl, combine the sweet potato, egg white, and ¼ cup of the panko.

3 Place the remaining ¼ cup panko on a plate. Form about 2 tablespoons of the sweet potato mixture into a nugget shape. Dredge in the panko to cover both sides of the nugget. Place on the prepared baking sheet. Repeat with the remaining sweet potato mixture to form 8 nuggets.

4 Bake until lightly browned, about 8 minutes per side. Cool and serve.

Makes 8 nuggets

MAKE AHEAD: Refrigerate for up to 3 days. Recrisp in a warm oven.

1 CUP MASHED SWEET POTATO

1 EGG WHITE, BEATEN

½ CUP PANKO BREAD CRUMBS

Nutrition per serving (1 nugget): 61 calories; 2g protein; 0g fat (0g sat. fat); 12g carbohydrates; 1g fiber; 2g sugars; 79mg sodium; 22mg calcium; 0.8mg iron; 86mg potassium; 2mg vitamin C; 2,773IU vitamin A

SMOOTHIE TIME

Like kids, teens, and grownups (so basically everyone), most older babies adore smoothies. Cool and creamy, they are fun to sip from a straw or even drink from a cup. Any of these smoothies can also be frozen into ice pops.

½ CUP UNSWEETENED COCONUT MILK BEVERAGE (FROM A CARTON, NOT A CAN)

½ CUP FROZEN MANGO

¼ CUP PLAIN FULL-FAT GREEK YOGURT

½ BANANA

½ TEASPOON GROUND TURMERIC

MANGO-BANANA TURMERIC

Place all the ingredients in a blender and blend until smooth.

Makes about 1⅓ cups (3 servings)

Nutrition per serving: 97 calories; 3g protein; 5g fat (2g sat. fat); 11g carbohydrates; 2g fiber; 7g sugars; 33mg sodium; 38mg calcium; 0.8mg iron; 141mg potassium; 22mg vitamin C; 1,235IU vitamin A

2 CUPS CUBED WATERMELON

¼ AVOCADO, PEELED

½ CUP FROZEN STRAWBERRIES

WATERMELON-STRAWBERRY

Place all the ingredients in a blender and blend until smooth.

Makes about 1¾ cups (3 servings)

Nutrition per serving: 65 calories; 1g protein; 3g fat (0g sat. fat); 11g carbohydrates; 2g fiber; 8g sugars; 2mg sodium; 13mg calcium; 0.4mg iron; 233mg potassium; 25mg vitamin C; 604IU vitamin A

CLOCKWISE FROM TOP LEFT:
MANGO-BANANA TURMERIC,
GREEN APPLE—SPINACH,
WATERMELON-STRAWBERRY

½ CUP WATER

½ GREEN APPLE, UNPEELED, CORED, AND CHOPPED

½ CUP BABY SPINACH

1 BANANA, SLICED AND FROZEN

GREEN APPLE–SPINACH

Place all the ingredients in a blender and blend until smooth.

Makes about 1½ cups (3 servings)

Nutrition per serving: 53 calories; 1g protein; 0g fat (0g sat. fat); 14g carbohydrates; 2g fiber; 8g sugars; 8mg sodium; 13mg calcium; 0.4mg iron; 173mg potassium; 8mg vitamin C; 653IU vitamin A

MAKE AHEAD: Refrigerate the Mango-Banana Turmeric and Watermelon-Strawberry smoothies for up to 24 hours. Shake or stir before serving. (The Green Apple–Spinach smoothie is best if sipped immediately.)

WHOLESOME TIP: To up the nutritional ante in any of these smoothies, add 1 tablespoon ground flaxseeds or an extra handful of baby spinach when blending.

My child always gets hungry when we're out of the house. Can you suggest some on-the-go snacks that I can toss in my bag as I run out the door?

Most single-ingredient fruits and vegetables are ideal for taking on the road. These recipes also make excellent out-of-the-house nibbles:

- Crinkle-Cut Carrots (page 72)
- Roasted Apple Slices (page 46)
- Cinnamon-Banana Pancakes (page 60)
- Broccoli and Ham Egg Muffins (page 96)
- Peanut Butter Mini Muffin Bites (page 104)
- Whole-Grain Zucchini Banana Bread (page 106)
- Zucchini Bread Waffles (page 124)
- Cauliflower-Kale Tots (page 119)
- Sweet Potato Hummus with dippers (page 98)

FRUITY POPS

Ice pops are a gift for teething babies. Small ice pop molds with rings for handles make it easy for beginning eaters to enjoy a cool treat. When peaches are out of season, I prefer using partially defrosted frozen peach slices instead of the rock-hard, tasteless specimens found at the supermarket.

1 Place all the ingredients in a medium bowl and mash with a fork or potato masher. Stir to combine evenly.

2 Transfer the fruit mixture to ice pop molds and freeze until solid, about 2 hours.

Makes 1 cup yogurt mixture
(yield will vary based on your molds)

½ CUP FINELY CHOPPED PEACHES

½ CUP RASPBERRIES

½ CUP PLAIN FULL-FAT GREEK YOGURT

Nutrition per serving (2 tablespoons): 51 calories; 3g protein; 4g fat (1g sat. fat); 3g carbohydrates; 1g fiber; 1g sugars; 25mg sodium; 17mg calcium; 0.3mg iron; 30mg potassium; 11mg vitamin C; 750IU vitamin A

PUMPKIN PIE POPS

Don't wait for fall to make these cool, creamy treats.
Canned pumpkin is in season any time of year.

¼ CUP UNSWEETENED
ALMOND MILK OR COCONUT
MILK BEVERAGE (FROM A
CARTON, NOT A CAN)

½ CUP CANNED PURE
PUMPKIN PURÉE

½ BANANA

PINCH OF GROUND NUTMEG

PINCH OF GROUND CINNAMON

1 Place all the ingredients in a blender in the order listed.
Blend until smooth.

2 Pour into ice pop molds and freeze until solid, at least
2 hours.

*Makes about 1 cup pumpkin mixture
(yield will vary based on your molds)*

Nutrition per serving (2 tablespoons): 15 calories; 0g protein;
0g fat (0g sat. fat); 3g carbohydrates; 1g fiber; 2g sugars; 6mg sodium;
7mg calcium; 0.3mg iron; 61mg potassium; 1mg vitamin C;
2,403IU vitamin A

CAULIFLOWER-KALE TOTS

These savory bites are perfect to take on the go.

1 Preheat the oven to 375°F. Line a baking sheet with parchment paper.

2 Place a steamer basket over 1 inch of water in a large saucepan. Bring the water to a boil. Add the cauliflower, cover the pan, and steam until tender, about 10 minutes. Cool for 10 minutes.

3 Place the kale in a food processor. Pulse until the kale is finely chopped. Add the cauliflower and egg and process until smooth. Transfer to a large bowl.

4 Add the panko, Italian seasoning (if using), and pepper. Stir to combine. Form the mixture into 12 tots, about 2 inches by 1 inch, and place them on the prepared baking sheet.

5 Drizzle the tots with half the olive oil and bake for 15 minutes. Gently flip the tots, drizzle with the remaining olive oil, and bake for 15 minutes more. Cool and serve.

Makes 12 servings

MAKE AHEAD: Bake these tots and refrigerate them up to 3 days in advance. Serve cold, at room temperature, or very gently warmed in the oven.

4 CUPS CAULIFLOWER FLORETS

2 CUPS PACKED CURLY KALE

1 EGG

½ CUP PANKO BREAD CRUMBS

½ TEASPOON SALT-FREE ITALIAN SEASONING (OPTIONAL)

FRESHLY GROUND BLACK PEPPER

1 TABLESPOON OLIVE OIL

Nutrition per serving (1 tot): 44 calories; 2g protein; 2g fat (0g sat. fat); 6g carbohydrates; 2g fiber; 1g sugars; 28mg sodium; 18mg calcium; 0.4mg iron; 25mg potassium; 17mg vitamin C; 1,378IU Vitamin A

GOLDEN CORN CAKES

These petite pancakes are bursting with summery flavor. If you have some around, add a handful of finely chopped fresh herbs like basil, mint, parsley, cilantro, or chives.

1 In a medium bowl, whisk together the flour, baking soda, and pepper. Stir in the eggs. Add the squash, corn, and feta (if using) and stir to combine.

2 Heat the olive oil in a medium skillet. Working in batches if necessary, drop heaping tablespoons of the batter into the oil. Cook until golden brown and cooked through, about 4 minutes per side. Transfer to a paper towel–lined plate and serve.

Makes 12 cakes

MAKE AHEAD: Refrigerate for up to 3 days. Serve cold, at room temperature, or gently warmed.

AGE IT UP: Add ½ teaspoon salt to the batter.

⅓ CUP ALL-PURPOSE FLOUR

¼ TEASPOON BAKING SODA

FRESHLY GROUND BLACK PEPPER

2 EGGS, BEATEN

2 CUPS GRATED YELLOW SUMMER SQUASH

¾ CUP FRESH OR FROZEN CORN KERNELS

¼ CUP CRUMBLED FETA CHEESE, OR MORE TO TASTE (OPTIONAL)

2 TABLESPOONS OLIVE OIL

Nutrition per serving (1 cake): 91 calories; 3g protein; 4g fat (1g sat. fat); 11g carbohydrates; 1g fiber; 0g sugars; 49mg sodium, 23mg calcium; 0.6mg iron; 91mg potassium; 3mg vitamin C; 124IU vitamin A

BAKED OATMEAL

This is a tricked-out version of the basic recipe on page 55. Not a blueberry fan? Swap in raspberries or chopped strawberries. Almond butter would make an admirable stand-in for the peanut butter.

1 TABLESPOON UNSALTED BUTTER, MELTED, PLUS MORE FOR THE PAN

2 CUPS ROLLED OATS

1 TEASPOON GROUND CINNAMON

1 TEASPOON BAKING POWDER

2 CUPS WHOLE MILK

1 EGG

¼ CUP PEANUT BUTTER

2 BANANAS, CUT INTO ½-INCH SLICES

½ CUP BLUEBERRIES

1 Preheat the oven to 400°F. Grease an 8 x 8-inch baking pan with butter.

2 In a large bowl, whisk together the oats, cinnamon, and baking powder. Whisk in the milk, butter, egg, and peanut butter.

3 Lay the banana slices over the bottom of the prepared pan in a single layer. Cover with the oat mixture. Dot with blueberries and bake until no longer jiggly in the center, 35 to 40 minutes.

4 Cool, chill for at least 2 hours, and cut into cubes.

Makes 12 servings

MAKE AHEAD: Refrigerate for up to 3 days.

AGE IT UP: Add ¼ teaspoon salt to the oat mixture before baking. Serve warm, drizzled with maple syrup.

Nutrition per serving: 194 calories; 8g protein; 7g fat (2g sat. fat); 26g carbohydrates; 4g fiber; 4g sugars; 100mg sodium; 67mg calcium; 1.5mg iron; 255mg potassium; 3mg vitamin C; 123IU vitamin A

BREAKFAST FOR BABY

10 easy options for the self-fed baby:

TOAST STICKS
spread with avocado, nut butter,
or a thin layer of ricotta cheese

DRY LOW-SUGAR CEREAL,
such as Cheerios

BAKED OATMEAL

THICK OATMEAL
(this will get messy!)

WHOLE-GRAIN PANCAKES OR WAFFLES

CHOPPED HARD-BOILED EGGS

ONE-EGG OMELET

Fruit and/or vegetable
SMOOTHIES

WHOLE-GRAIN, LOW-SUGAR MUFFINS

WHOLE-GRAIN MINI BAGELS,
lightly toasted

Don't forget a veggie! Get in the habit of offering your baby a vegetable at every meal, including breakfast.

Zucchini Bread
WAFFLES

I like to make a double batch of these subtly sweet waffles and freeze them for easy breakfasts.

1 CUP ALL-PURPOSE FLOUR

¾ SPELT FLOUR OR WHOLE-WHEAT PASTRY FLOUR

¼ CUP CORNSTARCH

¼ CUP SUGAR

1 TABLESPOON GROUND CINNAMON

2 TEASPOONS BAKING POWDER

½ TEASPOON GROUND NUTMEG

3 EGGS, BEATEN

1 CUP WHOLE MILK

4 TABLESPOONS UNSALTED BUTTER, MELTED

1 TABLESPOON VANILLA

2 CUPS GRATED ZUCCHINI

NONSTICK COOKING SPRAY

1 Preheat a waffle iron to medium-high.

2 In a large bowl, whisk together the flours, cornstarch, sugar, cinnamon, baking powder, and nutmeg. Add the eggs, milk, butter, and vanilla and stir to combine. Stir in the zucchini.

3 Spray the waffle iron with nonstick cooking spray. Ladle the batter into the waffle iron and cook until browned, 5 to 6 minutes. Repeat with the remaining batter.

4 Cool and cut into strips or small pieces.

Makes 10 waffles

MAKE AHEAD: Refrigerate for up to 3 days or freeze for up to 3 months. Whether refrigerated or frozen, I like to reheat waffles (and pancakes) in the toaster. It's quick, requires no dishes, and makes the waffle just a tiny bit crispy.

FREEZING TIP

To freeze, line a baking sheet with parchment paper and lay the waffles in flat layers, separating the layers with parchment. Freeze, then transfer to a zip-top freezer bag. This keeps the waffles from sticking together in the bag.

Nutrition per serving (1 waffle): 155 calories; 5g protein; 7g fat (4g sat. fat); 18g carbohydrates; 1g fiber; 4g sugars; 32mg sodium, 46mg calcium; 0.8mg iron; 158mg potassium; 4mg vitamin C; 307IU vitamin A

Rainbow Carrot and
QUINOA MASH

You are in control of how chunky this colorful and nutrient-rich dish is—smash the carrots more or less, depending on your baby's stage.

½ POUND CARROTS, PREFERABLY RAINBOW, CHOPPED INTO 2-INCH CHUNKS

2 TEASPOONS OLIVE OIL, PLUS MORE FOR SERVING

FRESHLY GROUND BLACK PEPPER

½ CUP COOKED QUINOA (SEE NOTE, RIGHT)

1 TEASPOON FRESH LIME JUICE

1 Preheat the oven to 425°F. Line a baking sheet with parchment paper.

2 Place the carrots on the prepared baking sheet and toss with the olive oil and a few grindings of pepper. Cover the pan tightly with aluminum foil and roast for 15 minutes. Remove the foil and roast for 15 minutes more. Cool slightly.

3 Cut the carrots into small chunks and mash with a fork. Combine with the quinoa and lime juice. Drizzle each serving with ¼ teaspoon olive oil.

4 Deliver this colorful and nutrient-rich dish with a spoon or let your baby pick it up in gobs.

Makes about 4 servings

MAKE AHEAD: Refrigerate for up to 3 days.

AGE IT UP: Skip mashing the carrots, and toss the carrot-quinoa mixture with chopped fresh cilantro and/or baby arugula for a sweet-savory salad. Season with salt and add more olive oil and lime juice, if you'd like.

TO COOK QUINOA: Bring 2 cups water to a boil in a small saucepan. Add 1 cup quinoa. Reduce the heat to low, cover, and cook until the quinoa is tender and the water has been absorbed, 12 to 15 minutes.

Nutrition per serving (¼ cup): 72 calories; 2g protein; 3g fat (0g sat. fat); 11g carbohydrates; 2g fiber; 3g sugars; 41mg sodium; 23mg calcium; 0.5mg iron; 223mg potassium; 4mg vitamin C; 9,474IU vitamin A

MIX IT UP

A grain and veggie combo, like in the Rainbow Carrot and Quinoa Mash recipe, opposite, plus fat and acid, is a tried-and-true culinary equation. Know the elements and you'll never be far from a wholesome dish for baby, a satisfying salad for you, or a crowd-pleasing side for family and friends.

1 CHOOSE OR INVENT A GRAIN AND VEGGIE COMBO:

Here are a few other combinations I like—but feel free to mix and match virtually any grain with any veggie.

- Farro + very finely chopped lacinato kale (cooked or raw)

- Wheat berries + roasted or steamed beets

- Rice + finely chopped broccoli

- Oats + roasted butternut squash (this is more of a porridge)

- Barley + roasted or blanched asparagus

For babies, make sure the grains and the veggies are very tender, and mash them together with a fork so your little one can pick up the meal by the handful. As your eaters age, feel free to leave both elements a little al dente and toss the grains and veggies together hot or cold like a salad.

2 ADD A FAT: Olive oil, avocado oil, walnut oil, or canola oil to help bind and flavor the dish

3 ADD AN ACID: Lemon juice, lime juice, or vinegar (such as apple cider, white wine, red wine, sherry, or balsamic vinegar)

For toddlers, big kids, and grownups continue to steps 4 and 5. If the dish is for baby, mix and serve.

4 ADD SEASONING: Salt and/or pepper

5 ADD EXTRAS: Capers, chopped fresh herbs, chopped olives, chopped nuts, chopped dried fruit, cheese, and/or toasted seeds

VEGGIE PARMESAN BREAD

Tote this savory snack to daycare or on the road. It also makes a satisfying breakfast.

NONSTICK COOKING SPRAY

1 CUP ALL-PURPOSE FLOUR

½ CUP CORNMEAL

½ CUP GRATED PARMESAN CHEESE

1 TABLESPOON BAKING POWDER

½ TEASPOON BAKING SODA

3 EGGS

1 CUP BUTTERMILK

⅓ CUP CANOLA OR OLIVE OIL

1 CUP GRATED ZUCCHINI

1 CUP CHOPPED COOKED SPINACH (I START WITH FROZEN, DEFROST, AND DRAIN WELL)

½ CUP GRATED CARROTS

1 Preheat the oven to 350°F. Spray a 9 x 5-inch loaf pan with cooking spray.

2 In a large bowl, whisk together the flour, cornmeal, Parmesan, baking powder, and baking soda.

3 In a small bowl, whisk together the eggs, buttermilk, and canola oil.

4 Add the wet ingredients to the dry ingredients and stir to combine. Stir in the zucchini, spinach, and carrots. Transfer to the prepared loaf pan.

5 Bake the bread for 45 minutes, or until a toothpick inserted into the center of the loaf comes out clean. Cool on a wire rack for 15 minutes. Remove the bread from the pan and cool completely on the rack.

6 To serve, slice and cube.

Makes 12 servings

MAKE AHEAD: Refrigerate for up to 3 days.

AGE IT UP: Add 1 teaspoon salt to the batter.

Nutrition per serving: 166 calories; 6g protein; 10g fat (2g sat. fat); 15g carbohydrates; 1g fiber; 1g sugars; 121mg sodium; 104mg calcium; 1.3mg iron; 159mg potassium; 2mg vitamin C; 2,840IU Vitamin A

CHICKEN QUESADILLA BITES

I like to serve this delicious meal with chopped tomato spritzed with lime juice. Think of it as baby's first salsa!

1 Spread the mashed avocado on the tortilla. Place the chicken on the bottom half of the tortilla and sprinkle with the cheese. Fold the top half of the tortilla over the bottom and press to adhere.

2 Heat the canola oil in a small skillet over medium-high heat. Add the quesadilla and cook until lightly browned on the first side, 30 seconds to 1 minute. Carefully flip and cook until the second side is lightly browned and the cheese has melted. Transfer to a paper towel to blot any excess oil. Cool and cut into bites or strips.

Makes 2 servings

MAKE AHEAD: Refrigerate for up to 3 days. Reheat gently in a dry skillet.

COOKING TIP: Any leftover bit of boneless, skinless chicken will work here. Or poach a chicken breast to use. Bring a medium saucepan of water to a boil. Add the chicken and reduce the heat until the water is barely simmering. Poach for 15 to 20 minutes, or until the chicken is cooked all the way through. (I simply use a fork and knife to check the thickest part of the breast.) Cool and shred.

1 TABLESPOON MASHED AVOCADO

ONE 6-INCH FLOUR TORTILLA, BRIEFLY WARMED IN THE MICROWAVE (ABOUT 10 SECONDS)

¼ CUP SHREDDED COOKED CHICKEN (SEE COOKING TIP)

1 TABLESPOON SHREDDED CHEDDAR OR MONTEREY JACK CHEESE

1 TABLESPOON CANOLA OIL

Nutrition per serving: 161 calories; 7g protein; 11g fat (2g sat. fat); 8g carbohydrates; 1g fiber; 1g sugars; 130mg sodium; 48mg calcium; 0.7mg iron; 92mg potassium; 1mg vitamin C; 53IU vitamin A

TOMATO-FENNEL SOUP

There's no law that says soup has to be hot. Serve your baby this veggie-ful meal chilled or at room temperature. Let him drink from a cup or practice his spoon skills.

2 TABLESPOONS OLIVE OIL

1 FENNEL BULB, CHOPPED (ABOUT 2 CUPS)

ONE 28-OUNCE CAN WHOLE TOMATOES

3 CUPS VEGETABLE BROTH

1 MEDIUM SWEET POTATO, PEELED AND CHOPPED

1 Heat the olive oil in a large saucepan over medium-low heat. Add the fennel and cook, stirring occasionally, until tender, about 10 minutes.

2 Add the tomatoes with their juices, the broth, and the sweet potato. Bring to a boil. Reduce the heat to maintain a simmer and cook, stirring occasionally, until the sweet potato is tender, about 30 minutes. Remove from the heat and cool for up to 30 minutes.

3 Transfer the soup to a blender. Blend until smooth, working in batches if necessary.

Makes 7½ cups

MAKE AHEAD: This soup keeps beautifully in the fridge or freezer. I like to freeze it in individual serving sizes for easy defrosting.

AGE IT UP: Add ½ teaspoon salt for a comforting family meal. Grilled cheese optional (see Waffled Grilled Cheese, page 135).

COOKING TIP: Be careful when blending hot liquids. Remove the plastic insert from the blender lid and cover the opening with a doubled-over kitchen towel. This will prevent a buildup of pressure inside the blender, which could lead to a messy—and painful—accident.

Nutrition per serving (½ cup): 44 calories; 1g protein; 2g fat (0g sat. fat); 7g carbohydrates; 2g fiber; 3g sugars; 231mg sodium; 26mg calcium; 0.6mg iron; 210mg potassium; 9mg vitamin C; 1,334IU vitamin A

WAFFLED GRILLED CHEESE

This sandwich technically makes four baby-size servings, or one baby-size portion and one adult-size portion. It's never too early to teach them to share!

1 Preheat the waffle iron to medium.

2 Spread one side of each slice of bread with the butter. Spread the pesto on the other side of each slice. Sandwich the cheese between the pesto-smeared sides of the bread, so the buttery sides will come in contact with the waffle iron.

3 Put the sandwich in the waffle iron, close the iron, and cook until the bread is just crisp and the cheese has melted, about 4 minutes. Cool and cut into small bites.

Makes 1 sandwich (4 baby-size servings)

2 SLICES WHOLE-WHEAT BREAD

1 TEASPOON UNSALTED BUTTER, AT ROOM TEMPERATURE

1 TABLESPOON PESTO, STORE-BOUGHT OR HOMEMADE, SUCH AS THE HEMP PESTO ON PAGE 149

⅓ CUP SHREDDED GRUYÈRE OR CHEDDAR CHEESE

Nutrition per serving: 166 calories; 5g protein; 11g fat (4g sat. fat); 13g carbohydrates; 2g fiber; 1g sugars; 211mg sodium; 77mg calcium; 1mg iron; 105mg potassium; 0mg vitamin C; 144IU vitamin A

FRIED RICE FRITTATA

Let's face it: rice, couscous, orzo, and the like are some of the worst mess-makers. This frittata solves the problem by flipping the ratio of typical fried rice (lots of rice, one or two eggs) on its head.

2 TABLESPOONS CANOLA OIL

2 SCALLIONS, FINELY CHOPPED

2 GARLIC CLOVES, FINELY CHOPPED

2 TABLESPOONS FINELY CHOPPED FRESH GINGER

2 CUPS COOKED WHITE OR BROWN RICE

10 EGGS, BEATEN

1 Preheat the oven to 350°F.

2 Heat the canola oil in a 10-inch oven-safe skillet over medium-low heat. Add the scallions, garlic, and ginger and cook, stirring, until fragrant, about 2 minutes. Add the rice, increase the heat to medium, and cook, stirring, for 2 minutes more.

3 Pour the eggs over the rice mixture and cook for 1 to 2 minutes. Transfer the pan to the oven and cook until the center of the frittata is set, about 20 minutes. Cool for at least 10 minutes, then cut into chunks and serve.

Makes 10 servings

MAKE AHEAD: Refrigerate for up to 3 days. Reheat gently in the microwave, or simply serve cold or at room temperature.

AGE IT UP: Add 1 teaspoon salt to the eggs before beating. Serve with Sriracha. I also like adding finely chopped kimchi with the rice.

IS RICE SAFE?

Some rice products have been found to contain relatively high levels of arsenic, but this doesn't mean your baby needs to skip rice altogether. The trick is to serve your little one a balanced diet. Rice cereal three times a day is excessive; a little rice once or twice a week is reasonable.

Nutrition per serving: 134 calories; 7g protein; 7g fat (2g sat. fat); 10g carbohydrates; 1g fiber; 0g sugars; 65mg sodium; 32mg calcium; 1mg iron; 93mg potassium; 1mg vitamin C; 353IU vitamin A

DRINK
DO'S AND DON'TS

Before age one, a baby's primary source of hydration is breastmilk or formula. But you should also introduce your baby to water when she begins solids.

DO put a sippy cup or small open cup of water on the high-chair tray whenever your baby is eating. You want her to become accustomed to the fresh, clean taste of good old H_2O. Around eight to ten months, most babies can move on to cups with straws.

DON'T stay in the sippy cup stage for too long, if at all, since it may impede oral-motor development. Once your baby is about a year old, if you haven't already, start giving her an open cup with just a little water. You'll be surprised at how quickly she masters it.

DON'T offer your baby any sugar-sweetened beverages, including juice cocktails, sports drinks, lemonade, sweet tea, and sodas.

DON'T offer your baby cow's milk as a beverage. It may be hard for him to digest and it is likely to fill him up so much that he'll reject breastmilk, formula, or solids. It's fine to use cow's milk in recipes, and once your baby is 12 months old, you may opt to switch from breastmilk or formula to whole cow's milk or fortified soy milk.

DON'T give your baby juice. The American Academy of Pediatrics recommends no juice for babies and a maximum of 4 ounces a day for toddlers. He's better off getting the goodness of fruit through fiber-packed whole oranges or apples, for example.

DO stick with water at snack time or when you're out and about.

chapter four

FAMILY MEALS

(8 months and up)

One of the best parts about baby-led feeding is that your baby can, from virtually the time he starts solids, eat many of the same foods as the rest of the family. All the recipes in this chapter were created with the entire family in mind, from baby to toddler to big kid to grownup. The flavors are varied and interesting, and the textures are appropriate for babies who have mastered or are working on their pincer grasp.

When you serve dinner, place a little of the family meal on your baby's tray. Make sure to cut foods into appropriate-size pieces and continue offering your baby a cup of water at each meal.

Eating with your baby is incredibly important. And when I say "eating with," I don't just mean sitting with your baby while he eats. Yes, that's important, too, since you never want to leave a baby alone while he's eating. And of course, you won't always eat when he does and you won't always eat the same things. But to raise a healthy, happy eater, *try to eat the same foods at the same time as much as possible.* Your baby will learn that you, his number one role model, enjoy healthy, flavorful foods. He'll see how you put food in your mouth, how you chew, how you use a napkin. He'll observe that you eat a variety of foods and sometimes don't finish it all.

And hopefully, he'll begin to understand that food belongs on the plate . . . not on the floor.

Another important reason to begin eating together now, whether it's breakfast, lunch, or dinner, is that it sets the stage for years of eating together as a family. It's never too early to begin this healthy habit. Research suggests that eating together as your children grow promotes healthy eating habits and also higher self-esteem in kids, better grades, and less anxiety.

No, family meal is not always a rosy, blissful time. It can be stressful, say, if your toddler refuses to stay in his high chair or your preschooler rejects every vegetable you've served over the past month. But eating together is a habit worth preserving. It really is a time to connect, to catch up, to enjoy each other's company. And that's what family is all about, right?

A NOTE ON SERVING SIZES

The serving sizes in this chapter are larger, geared more toward bigger kids and adults. So don't expect your baby to eat his whole "serving." Just save leftovers for lunch the next day or let the biggest eater at the table enjoy a little more.

A NOTE ON SALT

Since it is my hope that you will use these recipes long after your baby is a toddler and beyond, I have included salt as an optional ingredient. Once your baby is a year old, you may begin adding a little salt to recipes, if you'd like. The nutritional information in the recipes does not include the salt, nor any other optional ingredients.

Remember, family dinner doesn't have to be extravagant or time-consuming. A simple meal shared is all that matters.

STARTING WITH A SPOON

The best way to teach your baby to use a spoon is to start early, from the first weeks of starting solids, even if all your baby does is play with the utensil. First, allow her to "help" you feed her by grabbing the spoon while you are steering it. Next, hand your baby her own spoon, one with a short handle that's not too big or heavy for small hands. Finally, give plenty of practice with food that sticks easily to a spoon and is easy to transfer into her mouth. Greek yogurt, applesauce, thick oatmeal, mashed potatoes, and thick vegetable soups are all good options.

on the side

Side dishes do more than pull their own weight at the dinner table. They can add color, flavor, and nutrition (think veggies!) to your meal, plus ensure there is something on the table that everyone likes. Side dishes don't need to be complicated or fancy or even require a recipe, and leftovers are ideal. I often roast a big batch of veggies on the weekend and just heat it up for a simple side one or two nights that week. A few of my favorite easy side dishes:

- Steamed or roasted veggies (see pages 43 and 144 for directions and ideas)

- Brown or white rice topped with sliced scallions and a drizzle of soy sauce

- Small cups of soup

- Farro cooked in chicken broth

- Couscous

- Pickles

- Baked potatoes or sweet potatoes

- Sautéed and sliced chicken sausage

- Hard-boiled eggs

- Cut-up veggies (cooked, if appropriate), with or without a dip

- Applesauce

- Roasted Zucchini Sticks (page 52)

- Rosemary Roots (page 78)

- Golden Corn Cakes (page 121)

- Curried Cauliflower (page 108)

- Cauliflower-Kale Tots (page 119)

- Roasted Sweet Potatoes with Cilantro-Feta Drizzle (page 156)

- Broccoli Brooms (page 48)

I'M DELICIOUS ROASTED

HOW TO ROAST

Need a quick side dish? Roast a veggie. Roasting vegetables until tender and golden brown brings out the food's natural sugars, making it extra-tempting. To roast, preheat the oven to 425°F and line a baking sheet with parchment paper. Cut the vegetable into roughly equal-size pieces so they will cook at an even rate. Toss the veggie with olive oil and salt and pepper (if using). Lay the veggies in a single layer on the baking sheet. If the sheet is too crowded or the veggies overlap, they will steam, not roast, and that delectable browning won't occur. Roast until tender and browned; the time will vary based on the vegetable. Cool and serve, or refrigerate. Veggies that are champion roasters:

- Carrots
- Parsnips
- Broccoli
- Cauliflower
- Zucchini and summer squash

- Winter squash such as butternut, acorn, and delicata
- Eggplant
- Cherry tomatoes
- Green beans

- Potatoes
- Sweet potatoes

And don't forget fruit! Apples, pears, peaches, and even bananas take well to roasting. Their sugars intensify, making them even more delicious.

LAMB FLATBREAD PIZZA

Try goat cheese in place of the mozzarella if you prefer, or go halvsies as we often do at my house.

1 LARGE PREPARED FLATBREAD PIZZA CRUST (ABOUT 14 OZ.)

¼ CUP PLAIN FULL-FAT GREEK YOGURT

1 TABLESPOON OLIVE OIL

½ POUND GROUND LAMB

½ CUP CHOPPED ONION

2 GARLIC CLOVES, SLICED

¼ TEASPOON SALT (OPTIONAL)

1 TEASPOON LEMON ZEST

4 OUNCES MOZZARELLA CHEESE, TORN INTO PIECES

FRESHLY GROUND BLACK PEPPER

HANDFUL OF CHOPPED FRESH HERBS, SUCH AS PARSLEY, MINT, AND/OR DILL

1 Preheat the oven to 425°F. Line a baking sheet with aluminum foil or parchment paper.

2 Place the crust on the prepared sheet. Spread the yogurt evenly over the crust.

3 Heat the olive oil in a large skillet over medium heat. Add the lamb, onion, garlic, and salt (if using). Cook, breaking up the lamb with a spoon as it cooks, until the lamb is no longer pink and the onion is soft, about 5 minutes. Stir in the lemon zest.

4 Spoon the lamb mixture over the yogurt on the crust, leaving most of the fat behind in the pan. Top the lamb with the torn mozzarella and pepper to taste. Bake for 8 to 10 minutes, or until the cheese is melted and turning golden. Remove from the oven and top with the herbs. Let sit for at least 5 minutes before slicing into strips or small bites and serving.

Makes 4 servings

Nutrition per serving: 406 calories; 25g protein; 22g fat (7g sat. fat); 28g carbohydrates; 2g fiber; 2g sugars; 509mg sodium; 255mg calcium; 3mg iron; 192mg potassium; 6mg vitamin C; 495IU Vitamin A

TUSCAN TUNA PASTA SALAD

This savory salad also makes excellent lunchbox food.

¾ TEASPOON SALT, PLUS MORE FOR THE PASTA WATER (OPTIONAL)

4 OUNCES WHOLE-GRAIN PENNE

3 CUPS SMALL BROCCOLI FLORETS

ONE 14.5-OUNCE CAN LOW-SODIUM CANNELLINI BEANS, DRAINED, RINSED, AND PATTED DRY

3 TABLESPOONS OLIVE OIL

2 TABLESPOONS FRESH LEMON JUICE

ONE 5-OUNCE CAN TUNA, PREFERABLY PACKED IN OIL, DRAINED

2 TABLESPOONS CAPERS

2 TABLESPOONS CHOPPED FRESH SAGE

FRESHLY GROUND BLACK PEPPER

1 Bring a large pot of salted water to a boil. Cook the pasta according to the package directions. Three minutes before the pasta is ready, add the broccoli florets to the pot. When the pasta and broccoli are cooked, drain, rinse with cold water, and dry very well with paper towels.

2 In the meantime, place half the cannellini beans in a large bowl. Mash with a fork. Add the olive oil and lemon juice and stir with the fork to combine.

3 Add the pasta, remaining beans, tuna, capers, sage, salt (if using), and pepper to taste. Stir to combine.

MAKE AHEAD: Refrigerate for up to 3 days.

AGE IT UP: Adults and older children may appreciate a sprinkle of spicy red pepper flakes on top of the salad.

WHOLESOME TIP: Tuna is an excellent source of protein and crucial omega-3 fatty acids. While it can be relatively high in mercury, if you serve it to your baby no more than once a week, it's a smart addition to your little one's diet. Choose light canned tuna, instead of albacore, to reduce mercury exposure.

Nutrition per serving: 360 calories; 18g protein; 14g fat (2g sat. fat); 39g carbohydrates; 8g fiber; 2g sugars; 473mg sodium; 22mg calcium; 1.4mg iron; 83mg potassium; 25mg vitamin C; 34IU vitamin A

HEMP PESTO PASTA

Classic pesto is made with basil leaves and pine nuts, but the Italian sauce seems made for riffing. Hemp seeds are a protein-rich super-food perfect for pesto.

1 Bring a large pot of water to a boil.

2 To make the pesto, combine the garlic, parsley, hemp seeds, and Parmesan in a food processor and process until the parsley is finely chopped. Add the olive oil, lemon zest, and salt (if using), and process until smooth.

3 To make the pasta, cook the pasta in the boiling water according to the package directions. Two minutes before the pasta is done, add the peas. Drain, without shaking off too much of the water, and return the pasta and peas to the pot. Add ½ cup of the pesto and toss to combine (you will have some pesto left over). Divide among four serving plates, drizzle with olive oil, and season with salt (if using) and pepper.

Makes 4 servings pasta and 1 cup pesto

MAKE AHEAD: To store the remaining ½ cup pesto, pour a thin layer of olive oil over the top, cover, and then refrigerate or freeze.

For the pesto

1 GARLIC CLOVE, COARSELY CHOPPED

4 CUPS COARSELY CHOPPED FLAT-LEAF PARSLEY

½ CUP HEMP SEEDS

½ CUP GRATED PARMESAN CHEESE

½ CUP OLIVE OIL

ZEST OF ½ LEMON

½ TEASPOON SALT (OPTIONAL)

For the pasta

8 OUNCES FARFALLE OR OTHER SHORT PASTA SHAPE

1 CUP FROZEN PEAS

OLIVE OIL

SALT (OPTIONAL) AND FRESHLY GROUND BLACK PEPPER

Nutrition per serving (pasta and 2 tablespoons pesto):
447 calories; 16g protein; 21g fat (3g sat. fat); 50g carbohydrates; 5g fiber; 3g sugars; 148mg sodium; 120mg calcium; 5.4mg iron; 228mg potassium; 46mg vitamin C; 3,271IU vitamin A

POTATO FRITTATA
with Red Pepper Sauce

This flavorful sauce adds a pop of color and is an easy way to introduce babies to walnuts.

For the sauce

1 ROASTED RED BELL PEPPER (SEE COOKING TIP), SEEDED

½ CUP CHOPPED TOASTED WALNUTS (2 OUNCES)

1 Preheat the oven to 350°F.

2 To make the sauce, combine all the sauce ingredients in a food processor and process until smooth. Refrigerate until ready to serve.

3 To make the frittata, place the potatoes in a medium saucepan. Cover with an inch of water, add the salt (if using), and bring to a boil. Boil for 3 minutes, then drain.

4 In a large bowl, beat the eggs, milk, salt (if using), and black pepper to taste.

5 Heat the olive oil in a 10-inch broiler-safe pan over medium heat. Add the onion and cook, stirring occasionally, until soft, about 5 minutes. Add the partially cooked potato cubes and cook for another 2 minutes.

6 Pour the egg mixture into the pan and cook for 2 minutes. Sprinkle on the shredded cheese. Bake for 15 minutes.

7 Switch the oven to broil and broil the frittata until golden brown and no longer jiggly. Cool for at least 10 minutes.

8 Cut the frittata into cubes and serve with the sauce for dipping or smearing.

Makes 8 servings

MAKE AHEAD: Refrigerate the frittata for up to 3 days and the sauce for up to 2 days. Serve the frittata cold, gently heated, or at room temperature.

COOKING TIP: Use store-bought roasted red peppers, or roast and peel your own: Broil a whole red bell pepper until blackened on all sides. Transfer to a bowl, cover with plastic wrap, and let the pepper steam for 15 minutes. The charred skin should slide right off.

2 TABLESPOONS MAYONNAISE

1 TABLESPOON TOMATO PASTE

½ TEASPOON SALT (OPTIONAL)

For the frittata

3 SMALL RED POTATOES (ABOUT ¾ POUND), PEELED AND CUBED

1 TEASPOON SALT, PLUS MORE FOR THE COOKING WATER (OPTIONAL)

8 EGGS

½ CUP WHOLE MILK

FRESHLY GROUND BLACK PEPPER

2 TABLESPOONS OLIVE OIL

1 SMALL ONION, CHOPPED (ABOUT ¾ CUP)

1 CUP SHREDDED MANCHEGO CHEESE (2 OUNCES)

Nutrition per serving: 261 calories; 13g protein; 19g fat (6g sat. fat); 12g carbohydrates; 2g fiber; 2g sugars; 183mg sodium; 182mg calcium; 1.6mg iron; 381mg potassium; 29mg vitamin C; 139IU vitamin A

EASIEST *and* BEST ROAST CHICKEN

For extra flavor, add a tablespoon of chopped fresh rosemary, sage, or thyme to the butter mixture. Leftovers are so versatile: top a salad, fold into a quesadilla, stuff a burrito, or serve with pasta. To make your meal planning even easier, consider roasting two chickens at a time. It's barely more work, and you'll have plenty of chicken for at least two more meals later in the week.

2 TABLESPOONS UNSALTED BUTTER, AT ROOM TEMPERATURE

2 TEASPOONS DIJON MUSTARD

ONE 3- TO 4-POUND CHICKEN, GIBLETS REMOVED

1¼ TEASPOONS SALT (OPTIONAL)

FRESHLY GROUND BLACK PEPPER

½ LEMON

1 Preheat the oven to 450°F. Place a roasting rack in a large sauté pan, cast-iron skillet, or sturdy rimmed baking sheet.

2 In a small bowl, mash together the butter and mustard with a fork.

3 Place the chicken on the roasting rack, breast-side down. Sprinkle the bottom and sides of the chicken with about ½ teaspoon of the salt (if using) and pepper to taste. Flip the bird so it's breast-side up. Using your fingers, break through the skin to make small pockets at the base of the breasts and top of the legs. Divide the butter mixture between the pockets, pushing the butter over the flesh and under the skin with your fingers.

4 Place the lemon half in the chicken's cavity and tie the legs together with kitchen twine, if it's handy. (If not, don't worry about it.) Sprinkle the top of the chicken with the remaining ¾ teaspoon salt (if using) and pepper to taste.

5 Place the chicken in the oven and roast for 30 minutes. Reduce the oven temperature to 375°F and roast for 45 minutes more. Take the chicken's temperature by inserting an instant-read thermometer in a meaty part of the chicken's thigh. The chicken is ready once it hits 165°F. Continue roasting if it's not quite up to temp.

6 Remove the chicken from the oven and place on a cutting board. Cover loosely with aluminum foil and let rest for 15 minutes. Carve and serve, shredding or cutting baby's portion into small pieces.

Makes 6 servings

MAKE AHEAD: Refrigerate for up to 3 days.

Nutrition per serving: 332 calories; 26g protein; 24g fat (8g sat. fat); 0g carbohydrates; 0g fiber; 0g sugars; 137mg sodium; 16mg calcium; 1.2mg iron; 262mg potassium; 2mg vitamin C; 311IU vitamin A

SPICED LAMB MEATBALLS
with Cucumber-Yogurt Sauce

This flavorful meat mixture is also delicious shaped into patties and grilled. Just omit the egg.

For the sauce

¾ CUP PLAIN FULL-FAT GREEK YOGURT

½ CUP GRATED CUCUMBER

1 GARLIC CLOVE, MINCED

1 TEASPOON FRESH LEMON JUICE

¼ TEASPOON SALT (OPTIONAL)

FRESHLY GROUND BLACK PEPPER

For the meatballs

OLIVE OIL, FOR THE PAN

2 TEASPOONS GROUND CORIANDER

1 TEASPOON GROUND CUMIN

1 To make the sauce, combine all the sauce ingredients in a small bowl. Refrigerate until ready to serve.

2 To make the meatballs, preheat the oven to 450°F. Grease an 8 x 8-inch (or similar-size) baking dish with olive oil.

3 In a small bowl, stir together the coriander, cumin, salt (if using), ginger, cinnamon, cayenne (if using), and black pepper.

4 Crack the egg into a large bowl. Beat with a fork. Add the lamb, spice mixture, cilantro, and panko. Combine with a fork or your (clean!) hands.

5 Form the lamb mixture into 12 meatballs and place in the prepared baking dish in a grid pattern so the meatballs are nestled against the edge of the pan and one another. Bake until an instant-read thermometer inserted into the center of the largest meatball registers 165°F, about 20 minutes. Let cool for at least 5 minutes.

6 Cut the meatball into chunks. Serve with the cucumber sauce.

Makes 12 meatballs and 1 cup sauce

MAKE AHEAD: Refrigerate the meatballs for up to 3 days and the sauce for up to 1 day.

1 TEASPOON SALT (OPTIONAL)

½ TEASPOON GROUND GINGER

¼ TEASPOON GROUND CINNAMON

⅛ TEASPOON CAYENNE PEPPER (OPTIONAL)

FRESHLY GROUND BLACK PEPPER

1 EGG

1 POUND GROUND LAMB

¼ CUP CHOPPED FRESH CILANTRO

¼ CUP PANKO BREAD CRUMBS

Nutrition per serving (1 meatball and 1 tablespoon sauce):
143 calories; 9g protein; 10g fat (5g sat. fat); 3g carbohydrates;
0g fiber; 1g sugars; 52mg sodium; 37mg calcium; 0.8mg iron;
136mg potassium; 1mg vitamin C; 50IU vitamin A

ROASTED SWEET POTATOES
with Cilantro-Feta Drizzle

The recipe for this flavorful sauce comes from Natalia, the nutritional expert behind this book, and her information-packed blog at feedingbytes.com. I also like this sauce on top of eggs, chicken, fish, or roasted veggies or smeared on the Sweet Potato and Quinoa Burgers on page 177.

For the sweet potatoes

2 MEDIUM SWEET POTATOES, CUT INTO THIN WEDGES

1 TABLESPOON OLIVE OIL

¼ TEASPOON SALT (OPTIONAL)

For the drizzle

1 SMALL GARLIC CLOVE, MINCED

½ CUP CHOPPED FRESH CILANTRO AND/OR PARSLEY

¼ CUP OLIVE OIL

ZEST OF 1 LEMON

2 TABLESPOONS CRUMBLED FETA

1 TEASPOON FRESH LEMON JUICE

PINCH OF SALT

1 To make the sweet potatoes, preheat the oven to 425°F. Line a baking sheet with parchment paper.

2 Toss the sweet potato wedges with the olive oil and salt (if using). Placed on the prepared baking sheet and roast until tender and browned, 25 to 30 minutes, flipping halfway through.

3 In the meantime, to make the sauce, stir together all the drizzle ingredients in a small bowl.

4 Serve the sweet potatoes with the sauce spooned over or alongside for dunking.

Makes 4 servings sweet potato and ½ cup sauce

MAKE AHEAD: Make the sauce up to 24 hours ahead. Refrigerate and bring to room temperature before serving.

Nutrition per serving (sweet potatoes and 2 tablespoons sauce):
219 calories; 2g protein; 18g fat (3g sat. fat); 14g carbohydrates; 2g fiber; 3g sugars; 90mg sodium; 46mg calcium; 0.6mg iron; 237mg potassium; 3mg vitamin C; 9,376IU vitamin A

CREAMY CAULIFLOWER SOUP

Despite its name, there's actually no cream or dairy in this recipe. The magic ingredient? A potato! The humble spud gives this satisfying soup body and smoothness. Garnish with chopped chives, crumbled bacon, or croutons, if you'd like.

2 TABLESPOONS UNSALTED BUTTER

2 LEEKS, SLICED (ABOUT 2 CUPS)

7 CUPS CAULIFLOWER FLORETS (FROM ABOUT 1 MEDIUM HEAD)

4 CUPS LOW-SODIUM CHICKEN BROTH

1 MEDIUM RUSSET POTATO, PEELED AND CUT INTO CHUNKS

1 TEASPOON SALT (OPTIONAL)

2 TEASPOONS FRESH LEMON JUICE

FRESHLY GROUND BLACK PEPPER

1 Melt the butter in a large saucepan over medium-low heat. Add the leeks and cook until the leeks are very tender, about 12 minutes.

2 Add the cauliflower, broth, potato, and salt (if using). Bring to a boil. Reduce the heat, cover, and simmer for 20 minutes, or until the cauliflower is tender. Let cool for up to 30 minutes, stirring occasionally. Add the lemon juice and season with pepper.

3 Working in batches, transfer the soup to a blender and blend until smooth, taking care when blending hot liquids (see Cooking Tip).

Makes 8 cups (6 servings)

MAKE AHEAD: Like most soups, this one is actually better a day or more after it's made. Refrigerate for up to 3 days or freeze for up to 3 months.

COOKING TIP: Be careful when blending hot liquids. Remove the plastic insert from the blender lid and cover the opening with a doubled-over kitchen towel. This will prevent a buildup of pressure inside the blender, which could lead to a messy—and painful—accident.

Nutrition per serving: 135 calories; 7g protein; 5g fat (3g sat. fat); 18g carbohydrates; 5g fiber; 4g sugars; 94mg sodium; 54mg calcium; 1.7mg iron; 352mg potassium; 51mg vitamin C; 616IU vitamin A

Parmesan-Sage
BEEF MEAT LOAF

It's easy to cut this recipe in half to make only four servings. (Just start checking the internal temperature about 15 minutes earlier.) But making a larger meat loaf isn't any more trouble, and leftovers make for an easy lunch or dinner later in the week.

1 Preheat the oven to 375°F. Line a baking sheet with parchment paper.

2 Heat the olive oil in a small skillet over medium heat. Add the onion, reduce the heat to low, and cook until the onion is soft, about 8 minutes. Add the garlic and cook for 2 minutes more. Remove from the heat and let cool for a few minutes.

3 Crack the eggs into a large bowl and beat with a fork. Add the ground beef, bread, Parmesan, sage, lemon zest, salt (if using), and pepper to taste. Mix with a fork or your hands.

4 Tip the meat mixture onto the prepared baking sheet. With your (clean!) hands, shape the meat into a rough oval, about 2 inches high. Smear the meat loaf with the ketchup, covering the top and sides with a thin glaze.

5 Bake for 55 to 60 minutes, or until the internal temperature registers 165°F on an instant-read thermometer. Let sit for at least 5 minutes before slicing and serving. Cut or break slices into small bites for baby.

Makes 8 servings

MAKE AHEAD: Combine the meat mixture up to a day before baking and refrigerate. Leftovers can be refrigerated for up to 3 days.

Nutrition per serving: 404 calories; 21g protein; 32g fat (11g sat. fat); 6g carbohydrates; 1g fiber; 2g sugars; 197mg sodium; 119mg calcium; 2.7mg iron; 345mg potassium; 2mg vitamin C; 107IU vitamin A

1 TABLESPOON OLIVE OIL

1 MEDIUM ONION, CHOPPED (ABOUT 1 CUP)

2 GARLIC CLOVES, MINCED

2 EGGS

2 POUNDS GROUND BEEF

2 SLICES SANDWICH BREAD, TORN INTO VERY SMALL PIECES

¼ CUP PARMESAN CHEESE

2 TABLESPOONS CHOPPED FRESH SAGE

ZEST OF 1 LEMON

1½ TEASPOONS SALT (OPTIONAL)

FRESHLY GROUND BLACK PEPPER

1 TABLESPOON KETCHUP

BUTTERNUT SQUASH GALETTE

Pie for dinner? You bet! This impressive-looking savory pastry is easy to make thanks to refrigerated piecrusts.

2 REFRIGERATED PIECRUSTS

ALL-PURPOSE FLOUR, FOR DUSTING

1 TABLESPOON OLIVE OIL

4 TABLESPOONS GRATED PARMESAN CHEESE

12 OUNCES THINLY SLICED BUTTERNUT SQUASH

1 EGG, BEATEN

½ TEASPOON SALT, PREFERABLY SEA SALT (OPTIONAL)

FRESHLY GROUND BLACK PEPPER

A FEW THYME SPRIGS

1 Preheat the oven to 400°F. Line a baking sheet with parchment paper.

2 Layer the piecrusts one on top of the other and roll out on a lightly floured surface until the round is about 14 inches in diameter. Transfer to the prepared baking sheet.

3 Leaving about 1½ inches of space around the edges, brush the olive oil onto the crust and sprinkle with 2 tablespoons of the Parmesan. Shingle the butternut squash slices over the olive oil and cheese. Sprinkle with the remaining 2 tablespoons Parmesan.

4 Fold the edges of the piecrust over the filling, pinching or pleating the crust if you wish. Brush the crust edges with the beaten egg until it's mostly coated; you won't use all the egg.

5 Sprinkle the entire galette with the salt (if using), including the crust. Season with pepper and toss on a few thyme sprigs.

6 Bake until the crust is golden brown and the squash is tender, about 30 minutes. Remove the thyme sprigs, leaving behind whatever leaves have fallen on the surface of the galette.

7 Cool for 10 minutes or more, then slice into wedges or squares. Cut baby's portion into small bites.

Makes 6 servings

Nutrition per serving: 383 calories; 6g protein; 25g fat (6g sat. fat); 35g carbohydrates; 2g fiber; 1g sugars; 394mg sodium; 81mg calcium; 2.2mg iron; 248mg potassium; 12mg vitamin C; 6,077IU vitamin A

MOTHER-IN-LAW SALMON

My Italian-born mother-in-law, Iolanda, is an amazing cook. But like many instinctive cooks, she isn't much for measuring, so even though I've eaten this delicious salmon dish countless times, it took me a few tries to nail the proportions—experimentation that was well worth it.

1 POUND SALMON, CUT INTO 3 OR 4 FILLETS

¼ TEASPOON SALT (OPTIONAL)

FRESHLY GROUND BLACK PEPPER

1 TABLESPOON OLIVE OIL

1 TABLESPOON MAYONNAISE

1 TABLESPOON FRESH LEMON JUICE

2 TEASPOONS DIJON MUSTARD

2 TABLESPOONS FINELY CHOPPED FRESH FLAT-LEAF PARSLEY

2 GARLIC CLOVES, MINCED

1 Preheat the oven to 375°F. Line a baking sheet with parchment paper.

2 Place the salmon fillets on the parchment. Sprinkle with the salt (if using) and pepper to taste.

3 In a small bowl, stir together the olive oil, mayonnaise, lemon juice, and mustard. Stir in the parsley and garlic.

4 Spoon the olive oil mixture over the salmon fillets. Roast the fish until it flakes easily in the center when tested with a fork or knife, 12 to 15 minutes, depending on the thickness. Cool and flake with a fork for baby.

Makes 4 servings

COOKING TIP: If your salmon still has the skin on it, no problem. Once the fish is cooked you can lift the fillets up off the skin easily with a spatula, leaving the skin behind on the baking pan.

Nutrition per serving: 274 calories; 23g protein; 19g fat (4g sat. fat); 1g carbohydrates; 0g fiber; 0g sugars; 130mg sodium; 13mg calcium; 0.4mg iron; 422mg potassium; 6mg vitamin C; 57IU vitamin A

SMOKY TROUT CAKES

Smoked trout has long been one of my daughter's favorite fish. It has a savory, almost bacon-like flavor. Fish that tastes like bacon? Yes, please.

1 EGG

2 CUPS MASHED POTATO (FROM ABOUT 2 MEDIUM RUSSET POTATOES; SEE COOKING TIP)

ONE 10-OUNCE BOX FROZEN SPINACH, DEFROSTED AND WELL-DRAINED

6 OUNCES SMOKED TROUT, OIL (IF ANY) DRAINED OFF

¼ CUP PLAIN FULL-FAT GREEK YOGURT

2 SCALLIONS, FINELY CHOPPED

¾ TEASPOON SALT (OPTIONAL)

FRESHLY GROUND BLACK PEPPER

2 TABLESPOONS OLIVE OIL

1 Crack the egg into a large bowl. Beat with a fork. Add the mashed potato, spinach, smoked trout, yogurt, scallions, salt (if using), and pepper to taste. Mix with the fork until the ingredients are evenly distributed. Form the mixture into 8 cakes about 1 inch high.

2 Heat the olive oil in a large skillet over medium heat. Cook the cakes until golden brown, about 5 minutes per side. Cool and serve whole or cut into small pieces.

Makes 8 cakes

COOKING TIP: Use leftover mashed potatoes, or cook your own up to a day ahead. Bake potatoes for about 40 minutes in a 400°F oven, or prick with a fork and microwave for about 8 minutes, then peel and mash.

GET SAUCY

Stir together a lemony yogurt dip to serve alongside: ½ cup plain full-fat Greek yogurt, ½ teaspoon lemon zest, 1 tablespoon fresh lemon juice, ¼ teaspoon salt, and lots of freshly ground black pepper.

Nutrition per serving (1 cake): 260 calories; 11g protein; 6g fat (2g sat. fat); 17g carbohydrates; 2g fiber; 1g sugars; 544mg sodium; 74mg calcium; 2mg iron; 477mg potassium; 16mg vitamin C; 4,649 IU vitamin A

CHICKEN SALAD CUTLETS

My favorite chicken salad includes tender white meat chicken, walnuts, fruit, and a creamy mayo-based dressing. This dish has all the same elements, just rearranged. You'll see that there are no measurements for the ingredients in the simple salad dressing. Start with a little of everything, taste, and then adjust.

1 CUP WALNUTS

2 TABLESPOONS ALL-PURPOSE FLOUR

¼ TEASPOON SALT, PLUS MORE FOR THE SALAD (OPTIONAL)

FRESHLY GROUND BLACK PEPPER

1 POUND BONELESS, SKINLESS CHICKEN CUTLETS (ABOUT 4)

2 TABLESPOONS MAYONNAISE

2 TABLESPOONS OLIVE OIL, PLUS MORE FOR THE DRESSING

3 CUPS ARUGULA

1 RIPE PEACH, PITTED AND THINLY SLICED

FRESH LEMON JUICE

1 In a food processor, grind the walnuts with the flour until very finely chopped. The mixture should resemble bread crumbs. Transfer the mixture to a flat dish.

2 Sprinkle the cutlets on both sides with the salt (if using) and pepper to taste. Smear the mayonnaise over both sides of the cutlets. Dredge the cutlets in the walnut meal, pressing to help the "crumbs" adhere.

3 Heat the olive oil in a large skillet over medium heat. Working in batches, if necessary, to avoid crowding the pan, cook the cutlets until lightly browned and cooked through, about 4 minutes per side.

4 In a small bowl, toss together the arugula, peach slices, a drizzle of olive oil, a squeeze of lemon juice, and salt (if using) and pepper to taste. For adults and big kids, serve the salad on top of the cutlets. For babies, cool and cut the chicken into small bites or strips. Serve with the peach slices and salad.

Makes 4 servings

Nutrition per serving: 423 calories; 29g protein; 23g fat (2.3g sat. fat); 11g carbohydrates; 3.4g fiber; 4.4g sugars; 96mg sodium; 47mg calcium; 1mg iron; 223mg potassium; 5mg vitamin C; 482IU vitamin A

TOFU PARM

This vegetarian dinner takes a little bit of time to cook, but it's almost all hands-off. If you're in a rush, shorten (or skip) the marinating time.

1 To press the tofu, place the tofu block on a plate lined with a few folded paper towels. Cover the tofu with more paper towels. Place another plate on top and weigh it down with something heavy like a box of chicken broth or a can of tomatoes. Let the tofu drain for 20 minutes.

2 Preheat the oven to 425°F. Line a baking sheet with parchment paper.

3 In an 8 x 8-inch or similar-size baking dish, whisk together the olive oil, lemon juice, Italian herb blend, and pepper.

4 Cut the tofu into four equal-size rectangles. Place in the lemon mixture. Marinate for 20 minutes, flipping the tofu pieces after 10 minutes.

5 Transfer the tofu pieces to the prepared baking sheet, sprinkling the salt (if using) evenly on both sides of each piece. (Reserve the baking dish you used for marinating.) Bake the tofu until lightly browned, about 30 minutes, flipping them after 15 minutes.

6 Wipe out the baking dish you used for marinating the tofu. Pour in ¼ cup of the marinara sauce and spread it evenly over the bottom. Place the browned tofu in the marinara sauce. Cover with the remaining ½ cup sauce and the Parmesan. Bake for 10 minutes. Cool and cut the tofu into cubes to serve.

Makes 4 servings

Nutrition per serving: 182 calories; 10g protein; 13g fat (2g sat. fat); 9g carbohydrates; 2g fiber; 5g sugars; 198mg sodium; 239mg calcium; 2.2mg iron; 323mg potassium; 3mg vitamin C; 361IU vitamin A

1 POUND EXTRA-FIRM TOFU

2 TABLESPOONS OLIVE OIL

1 TABLESPOON FRESH LEMON JUICE

½ TEASPOON ITALIAN HERB BLEND

FRESHLY GROUND BLACK PEPPER

½ TEASPOON SALT (OPTIONAL)

¾ CUP MARINARA SAUCE

1 TABLESPOON GRATED PARMESAN CHEESE

ONE-PAN GNOCCHI

When you cook your entire dinner in the oven on a sheet-pan, cleanup is a snap. If you opt not to use the pancetta, increase the olive oil to 3 tablespoons and the salt (if using) to ½ teaspoon.

14 OUNCES MUSHROOMS, SUCH AS BABY BELLAS, OR A MIX

1 POUND SHELF-STABLE GNOCCHI

2 SHALLOTS, QUARTERED

2 OUNCES THICK-CUT PANCETTA, DICED (OPTIONAL)

2 TABLESPOONS OLIVE OIL

2 TEASPOONS FRESH THYME LEAVES

¼ TEASPOON SALT (OPTIONAL)

FRESHLY GROUND BLACK PEPPER

1 TABLESPOON BALSAMIC VINEGAR

1 Preheat the oven to 425°F. Line a baking sheet with parchment paper.

2 Halve or quarter the mushrooms so they are all about the same size. Place in a large bowl with the gnocchi, shallots, pancetta (if using), olive oil, thyme, salt (if using), and pepper to taste. Toss to combine. Transfer to the prepared baking sheet.

3 Roast for 25 minutes, stirring once about halfway through. Add the vinegar, stirring so it is evenly distributed. Cook for 3 minutes more.

4 To serve, halve or quarter the gnocchi depending on the size.

Makes 4 servings

Nutrition per serving: 448 calories; 18g protein; 16g fat (4g sat. fat); 67g carbohydrates; 1g fiber; 4g sugars; 155mg sodium; 25mg calcium; 4.5mg iron; 574mg potassium; 3mg vitamin C; 118IU vitamin A

Roasted Veggie
TOMATO SAUCE

This is a great sauce recipe to have in your arsenal. Serve it over pasta, as a dip, or on top of meatballs. I like to make a double batch and store extra in the freezer.

1 Preheat the oven to 425°F. Line a baking sheet with parchment paper.

2 Place the carrots, onion, bell pepper, and garlic on the prepared baking sheet. Toss with the olive oil. Cover with aluminum foil and roast for 10 minutes. Remove the foil and roast for 20 to 25 minutes more, or until the vegetables are tender. (If the garlic is browning too quickly, remove it a few minutes early with tongs.) Cool for 10 minutes.

3 Place the drained tomatoes and salt (if using) in a blender. Add the roasted vegetables. Blend until smooth.

Makes 4 cups

MAKE AHEAD: Refrigerate for up to 5 days.

2 CARROTS, CUT INTO 1-INCH CHUNKS

1 YELLOW ONION, TRIMMED AND QUARTERED (OR CUT INTO EIGHTHS, IF LARGE)

1 RED BELL PEPPER, CORED AND QUARTERED

2 GARLIC CLOVES

1 TABLESPOON OLIVE OIL

ONE 28-OUNCE CAN DICED TOMATOES, DRAINED

¾ TEASPOON SALT (OPTIONAL)

Nutrition per serving (½ cup): 52 calories; 1g protein; 2g fat (0g sat. fat); 9g carbohydrates; 3g fiber; 5g sugars; 208mg sodium; 26mg calcium; 0.5mg iron; 103mg potassium; 28mg vitamin C; 3,408IU vitamin A

SHRIMP SLIDERS

If I don't have slider buns on hand or can't find them at the store, I cut brioche hot dog buns into thirds. They are the perfect size, taste delish brushed with melted butter, and almost convince me I'm eating a shrimp roll at the shore.

1 POUND LARGE SHRIMP, PEELED AND CLEANED

½ CUP PANKO BREAD CRUMBS

¼ CUP MAYONNAISE

¼ CUP CHOPPED FRESH CHIVES

ZEST OF 1 LEMON

1 TABLESPOON FRESH LEMON JUICE

½ TEASPOON CELERY SEEDS

¼ TEASPOON SALT (OPTIONAL)

FRESHLY GROUND BLACK PEPPER

2 TABLESPOONS UNSALTED BUTTER, PLUS MORE FOR THE BUNS IF DESIRED

8 SLIDER BUNS, TOASTED

1. Place the shrimp in a food processor and pulse until almost a paste. It's okay if there are a few larger pieces. Transfer the shrimp to a large bowl.

2. Add the panko, mayonnaise, chives, lemon zest, lemon juice, celery seeds, salt (if using), and pepper to taste and stir to combine. Form the shrimp mixture into 8 patties.

3. Melt the butter in a large skillet over medium heat. Cook the sliders for 3 to 4 minutes per side, or until cooked through.

4. Serve on toasted slider buns, brushed with melted butter, if desired. Cut the sandwich into small pieces. Yes, your baby will probably remove the shrimp cake from the bun, and that's A-OK.

Makes 8 sliders

Nutrition per serving (1 slider and bun): 207 calories; 12g protein; 5g fat (2g sat. fat); 27g carbohydrates; 1g fiber; 0g sugars; 574mg sodium; 113mg calcium; 1.4mg iron; 71mg potassium; 2mg vitamin C; 58IU vitamin A

Butternut Squash
MAC 'N' CHEESE

Incorporating a puréed vegetable into a pasta dish or other sauce is a popular way of "sneaking" veggies into kids' food. I'm not a fan of the tactic, preferring instead to help teach kids to like a wide variety of foods over the long run. The puréed butternut squash in this crowd-pleasing dish isn't hidden—it adds color and flavor (and nutrition!) that deserves to be celebrated, not concealed.

1 Preheat the oven to 375°F. Butter a 9 x 13-inch baking dish. Bring a large pot of water to a boil.

2 In a medium saucepan, bring 1 inch of water to a simmer. Place a steamer basket over the water. Add the butternut squash. Cover and steam until tender, 12 to 15 minutes. Transfer to a bowl and mash well with a fork or potato masher. You should have about 2 cups.

3 Cook the pasta according to the package directions, drain, and return the pasta to the pot.

4 Melt the butter in a medium saucepan over medium heat. Add the flour and whisk until smooth and bubbling. Cook for 2 minutes or until the mixture is a light tan. Whisk in the milk. Bring the mixture to a simmer, whisking frequently. Cook for 2 minutes, then remove the pan from the heat. Whisk in the mashed butternut squash and salt (if using). Stir in the Gruyère and cream cheese.

5 Pour the cheese sauce over the pasta, and stir to combine.

6 Transfer the mixture to the prepared baking pan. Top evenly with the panko and Parmesan. Bake until golden brown, about 30 minutes.

½ CUP (1 STICK) UNSALTED BUTTER, PLUS MORE FOR THE BAKING DISH

1 POUND CUBED BUTTERNUT SQUASH (3 CUPS)

1 POUND CAVATAPPI OR OTHER MEDIUM-LENGTH PASTA

⅓ CUP ALL-PURPOSE FLOUR

2 CUPS WHOLE MILK

1¼ TEASPOONS SALT (OPTIONAL)

2 CUPS SHREDDED GRUYÈRE OR CHEDDAR CHEESE (ABOUT 4 OUNCES)

INGREDIENTS CONTINUE

½ CUP CREAM CHEESE
(4 OUNCES)

¼ CUP PANKO BREAD CRUMBS

2 TABLESPOONS GRATED
PARMESAN CHEESE

7 To serve, cool and cut into bites.

Makes 8 servings

MAKE AHEAD: There are several ways to get a head start on this dish. Steam and mash the squash and/or cook the pasta up to 3 days in advance and refrigerate. Alternatively, assemble the whole dish up to 24 hours ahead, cover, refrigerate, and bake just before serving , adding a few minutes of cooking time. Reheat leftovers in the oven or microwave.

GET A HEAD START

If I have one dinner mantra it's this: Make-ahead, make-ahead, make-ahead. This doesn't always mean making the whole dinner ahead of time, although that's certainly a lifesaver on many nights. But to me, make-ahead means preparing any component of dinner—whether large or small—in advance. This might look like:

- Washing kale or lettuce over the weekend so it's always ready for a salad.

- Washing and prepping veggies, such as broccoli, cauliflower, or green beans, so they're ready to cook. I find that the washing and prepping take more active time than actually roasting, steaming, or blanching the vegetables.

- Chopping the onion and garlic for meat loaf or meatballs.

- Stirring together the dry ingredients for pancakes, waffles, or muffins. (I often do this on a Friday night so breakfast is quicker the next morning.)

- Making marinara sauce or pesto to have on-hand in the fridge or freezer.

Nutrition per serving: 544 calories; 16g protein; 24g fat (14g sat. fat); 60g carbohydrates; 4g fiber; 6g sugars; 215mg sodium; 251mg calcium; 2.7mg iron; 351mg potassium; 12mg vitamin C; 6,409IU vitamin A

Sweet Potato and
QUINOA BURGERS

You can certainly fry these up as little cakes or sliders, but I like to serve them as fat burgers atop toasted English muffins with a smear of pesto, chimichurri, or the cilantro-feta drizzle on page 156.

1 Break the egg into a large bowl and beat with a fork. Add the mashed sweet potato, quinoa, parsley, salt (if using), and pepper to taste. Form the mixture into 4 burgers about 1 inch thick.

2 Heat the olive oil in a large skillet over medium heat. Working in batches if necessary, cook the burgers until well browned, about 5 minutes per side. Cool for 5 to 10 minutes before serving. The burgers will firm up as they cool. Cut into small pieces to serve.

Makes 4 servings

MAKE AHEAD: Cook the quinoa and/or sweet potatoes up to 2 days ahead and refrigerate. Refrigerate cooked burgers for up to 3 days.

COOKING TIP: For the mash, roast whole sweet potatoes in a 425°F oven for about 50 minutes, or prick with a fork and microwave for 7 to 8 minutes.

1 EGG

1 CUP MASHED SWEET POTATO (FROM 1 LARGE OR 2 MEDIUM SWEET POTATOES; SEE COOKING TIP)

1½ CUPS COOKED QUINOA (SEE PAGE 127)

½ CUP FINELY CHOPPED FRESH FLAT-LEAF PARSLEY

¾ TEASPOON SALT (OPTIONAL)

FRESHLY GROUND BLACK PEPPER

2 TABLESPOONS OLIVE OIL

Nutrition per serving: 221 calories; 6g protein; 9g fat (2g sat. fat); 29g carbohydrates; 4g fiber; 5g sugars; 42mg sodium; 40mg calcium; 1.9mg iron; 323mg potassium; 11mg vitamin C; 12,970 IU vitamin A

CRISPY COCONUT COD

Use this same breading and baking technique with chicken tenders, shrimp, or zucchini. Don't forget the dipping sauce!

2 TABLESPOONS KETCHUP

1 TABLESPOON SWEET CHILI SAUCE

½ CUP ALL-PURPOSE FLOUR

1 EGG

½ CUP PANKO BREAD CRUMBS

¼ CUP UNSWEETENED SHREDDED COCONUT

¾ POUND COD, CUT INTO 2 x ½-INCH RECTANGLES

¼ TEASPOON SALT (OPTIONAL)

NONSTICK COOKING SPRAY, PREFERABLY COCONUT OIL SPRAY

1 Preheat the oven to 375°F. Line a baking sheet with parchment paper.

2 In a small bowl, stir together the ketchup and sweet chili sauce. Refrigerate until ready to serve.

3 Set out three shallow plates or bowls. Place the flour on one, the egg in another, and the panko and coconut on the third. Beat the egg, and stir together the panko and coconut.

4 Sprinkle the cod pieces with the salt (if using) on both sides. Dredge one piece of the cod in the flour, shaking off excess. Coat with the egg, letting any excess drip off, and then dredge in the panko-coconut mixture, pressing so the crumbs adhere. Place the breaded cod on the prepared baking sheet. Continue with the remaining cod pieces. Lightly spray both sides of each piece with coconut oil or other nonstick cooking spray.

5 Bake for 10 minutes, or until the fish flakes easily with a fork, flipping each piece halfway through.

6 Flake the fish and serve with the sweet chili-ketchup dipping sauce.

Makes 4 servings

Nutrition per serving: 256 calories; 19g protein; 4g fat (2g sat. fat); 18g carbohydrates; 1g fiber; 5g sugars; 265mg sodium; 27mg calcium; 0.9mg iron; 442mg potassium; 2mg vitamin C; 185IU vitamin A

Juicy Lucy
TURKEY MEATBALLS

An ooey-gooey cheesy center takes these meatballs from good to great. Serve them plain or with Roasted Veggie Tomato Sauce (page 171).

---

1 Preheat the oven to 450°F. Grease a medium-size baking dish with olive oil.

2 Crack the egg into a large bowl and beat with a fork. Add the turkey, bread crumbs, parsley, salt (if using), garlic powder, and pepper to taste. Mix well.

3 Form the meat mixture into 12 meatballs. Press your thumb into each meatball to make an indentation. Push a mozzarella cube into the indentation in each meatball and re-form the meat into a ball so the cheese is completely enclosed.

4 Place the meatballs in the baking dish. Bake until an instant-read thermometer inserted into the center of a meatball registers 165°F, 20 to 25 minutes. Cool and cut into small chunks to serve.

MAKE AHEAD: Form the meatballs up to 24 hours before baking and refrigerate. Refrigerate cooked meatballs for up to 3 days.

COOKING TIP: Shape the meatballs with wet hands. The meat will be much less sticky.

OLIVE OIL, FOR THE BAKING DISH

1 EGG

1 POUND GROUND TURKEY, PREFERABLY DARK MEAT

⅓ CUP DRY BREAD CRUMBS

1 TABLESPOON FINELY CHOPPED FLAT-LEAF PARSLEY

¾ TEASPOON SALT (OPTIONAL)

½ TEASPOON GARLIC POWDER

FRESHLY GROUND BLACK PEPPER

TWELVE ¼-INCH MOZZARELLA CUBES (1 OUNCE)

Nutrition per serving: 179 calories; 15g protein; 11g fat (3g sat. fat); 5g carbohydrates; 0g fiber; 0g sugars; 92mg sodium; 67mg calcium; 1.2mg iron; 170mg potassium; 1mg vitamin C; 192IU vitamin A

FRENCH LENTIL STEW

Let your baby eat this thick soup with a spoon or pick it up by the fistful. Lentils are an incredible source of protein, fiber, and iron. I like to serve this with crumbled bacon on top, or go the opposite direction and make this soup meatless by swapping out the chicken broth for vegetable broth.

2 TABLESPOONS OLIVE OIL

1 MEDIUM ONION, CHOPPED

2 CARROTS, CHOPPED

1 CELERY STALK, CHOPPED

4 CUPS LOW-SODIUM CHICKEN BROTH

1 CUP FRENCH (DU PUY) LENTILS, RINSED AND DRAINED

¾ TEASPOON SALT (OPTIONAL)

3 SMALL RED POTATOES (ABOUT 1 LB.), PEELED AND CHOPPED

¼ CUP CHOPPED PARSLEY

½ TEASPOON SHERRY VINEGAR

FRESHLY GROUND BLACK PEPPER

1 Heat the olive oil in a medium saucepan over medium heat. Add the onion, carrots, and celery. Reduce the heat to low and cook, stirring, until the vegetables are soft, 10 minutes.

2 Add the broth and bring to a boil. Add the lentils and salt (if using). Reduce the heat to maintain a simmer, cover, and cook for 30 minutes.

3 Add the potatoes and simmer, uncovered, for 20 minutes more.

4 Stir in the parsley, vinegar, and pepper to taste. Cool to just warm and serve.

Makes 6 servings

INGREDIENT TIP: French lentils, or lentilles du Puy, are small, greenish lentils that keep their shape when cooked.

MAKE AHEAD: This soup tastes even better a day or two after it's made. Refrigerate leftovers for up to 3 days.

Nutrition per serving: 271 calories; 15g protein; 6g fat (1g sat. fat); 41g carbohydrates; 13g fiber; 4g sugars; 89mg sodium; 55mg calcium; 3.8mg iron; 971mg potassium; 25mg vitamin C; 3,652IU vitamin A

GRAPEFRUIT SCALLOPS

Scallops are so quick to cook, but sometimes less tasty than they should be. The tricks to making sure they're delicious are to pat them dry before cooking and to wait until they've had a chance to form a savory brown crust before flipping them.

1 TEASPOON GRAPEFRUIT ZEST

¼ CUP FRESH GRAPEFRUIT JUICE

3 TABLESPOONS OLIVE OIL

¼ TEASPOON SALT, PLUS A PINCH (OPTIONAL)

1 POUND SCALLOPS, RINSED, PATTED DRY, AND SMALL, RECTANGULAR MUSCLE REMOVED

FRESHLY GROUND BLACK PEPPER

2 TABLESPOONS CHOPPED FRESH BASIL

1 In a flat baking dish, combine the grapefruit zest, grapefruit juice, 2 tablespoons of the olive oil, and a pinch of salt (if using). Whisk to combine. Add the scallops and turn to coat. Cover and refrigerate for up to 15 minutes.

2 Pat the scallops dry and season with the salt (if using) and pepper to taste, taking care to season both sides of each scallop.

3 Heat the remaining 1 tablespoon olive oil in a large, preferably nonstick, skillet over medium-high heat. Cook the scallops until golden brown, 3 to 4 minutes per side. Cut the scallops into small bites and serve topped with the chopped basil.

Makes 4 servings

Nutrition per serving: 176 calories; 14g protein; 11g fat (2g sat. fat); 6g carbohydrates; 0g fiber; 1g sugars; 446mg sodium; 32mg calcium; 1.5mg iron; 285mg potassium; 6mg vitamin C; 13IU vitamin A

CHICKEN CHILI

This hearty chili isn't very brothy, so it's easy for little ones to pick out soft chunks of chicken, tomatoes, or beans. Feel free to use leftover cooked chicken or the meat from a rotisserie bird.

2 BONE-IN, SKIN-ON CHICKEN BREASTS (ABOUT 1.5 POUNDS)

SALT AND FRESHLY GROUND BLACK PEPPER (OPTIONAL)

2 TABLESPOONS CANOLA OIL

1 MEDIUM ONION, CHOPPED

1 YELLOW BELL PEPPER, CHOPPED INTO LARGE CHUNKS (ABOUT ¾ CUP)

1 JALAPEÑO PEPPER, FINELY CHOPPED (OPTIONAL)

1 TEASPOON GROUND CUMIN

½ TEASPOON CHILI POWDER

1. Preheat the oven to 400°F. Line a baking sheet with parchment paper or aluminum foil.

2. Place the chicken breasts skin-side up on the prepared baking sheet, pat dry with paper towels, and sprinkle on both sides with salt and black pepper (if using). Roast until cooked through, about 35 minutes. Let cool. Remove and discard the skin and bones. Shred or chop the meat. You should have about 2 cups.

BE PREPARED

Having these pantry and freezer staples on hand can help make mealtime easier:

- Good-quality marinara sauce (no added sugars)
- Canned or boxed tomatoes
- Tomato paste
- Canned beans
- Chicken and/or vegetable broth (low-sodium)
- A variety of rice, noodles, and pastas

- Panko bread crumbs
- Frozen vegetables (including cooked spinach and puréed squash)
- Frozen pizza dough (white or whole wheat)

3 Heat the canola oil in a large saucepan. Add the onion and bell pepper. Reduce the heat to medium-low and cook the vegetables, stirring occasionally, for 10 minutes, or until tender. Add the jalapeño and cook for 2 minutes. Add the cumin and chili powder and cook for 1 minute.

4 Add the tomatoes, broth, beans, and ¾ teaspoon salt (if using) to the pot. Bring to a boil. Reduce the heat to maintain a simmer and cook, partially covered, for 15 minutes.

5 Remove the chili from the heat. Stir in the chicken and cilantro.

6 Cool to just warm and serve with a spoon, but don't be surprised if your baby dives in with her hands.

Makes 6 servings (6 cups)

MAKE AHEAD: Refrigerate for up to 3 days.

ONE 28-OUNCE CAN DICED TOMATOES

1 CUP LOW-SODIUM CHICKEN BROTH

ONE 14.5-OUNCE CAN LOW-SODIUM CANNELLINI BEANS, DRAINED AND RINSED

¼ CUP CHOPPED FRESH CILANTRO

Nutrition per serving (1 cup): 334 calories; 39g protein; 6g fat (1g sat. fat); 23g carbohydrates; 5g fiber; 5g sugars; 523mg sodium; 45mg calcium; 0.8mg iron; 442mg potassium; 36mg vitamin C; 337IU vitamin A

Roasted
RATATOUILLE PASTA

Ratatouille, with its brightly colored veggies, is like summer on a plate. But by roasting the vegetables you can coax a lot of flavor out of even dead-of-winter produce.

1 TABLESPOON OLIVE OIL, PLUS MORE FOR THE PAN

1 MEDIUM YELLOW SQUASH OR ZUCCHINI, CUT INTO 1-INCH CHUNKS, ABOUT 2 CUPS

2 CUPS 1-INCH EGGPLANT CHUNKS

½ BELL PEPPER, CUT INTO 1-INCH CHUNKS

¾ TEASPOON SALT (OPTIONAL)

FRESHLY GROUND BLACK PEPPER

2 CUPS CHERRY TOMATOES, HALVED

6 OUNCES ORECCHIETTE OR OTHER SMALL PASTA

GRATED PARMESAN CHEESE, FOR SERVING (OPTIONAL)

1 Preheat the oven to 400°F. Grease a 9 x 13-inch baking pan with olive oil. Bring a large pot of water to a boil.

2 Place the squash, eggplant, and bell pepper in the prepared pan. Toss with the olive oil, ½ teaspoon of the salt (if using), and pepper to taste. Roast for 10 minutes. Add the cherry tomatoes, stir, and roast for 20 minutes more.

3 In the meantime, cook the orecchiette in the boiling water according to the package directions. Drain, taking care not to shake off all the cooking liquid.

4 Stir the cooked pasta into the ratatouille. Season with the remaining ¼ teaspoon salt (if using). Cool and serve, sprinkled with Parmesan and an extra drizzle of olive oil, if desired.

Makes 4 servings

MAKE AHEAD: The roasted vegetables freeze well, or refrigerate them for up to a day before tossing with the pasta.

Nutrition per serving: 218 calories; 7g protein; 5g fat (1g sat. fat); 40g carbohydrates; 5g fiber; 5g sugars; 10mg sodium; 18mg calcium; 2.1mg iron; 255mg potassium; 34mg vitamin C; 803IU vitamin A

SPAGHETTI SQUASH BAKE

On its own, spaghetti squash is a tad bland. But mixed with savory Parmesan and tangy marinara, it becomes crave-worthy. The cayenne pepper adds a hint of heat without being overpowering.

1 Preheat the oven to 400°F.

2 Cut the squash in half lengthwise and scrape out the seeds. Rub the flesh with a little olive oil and place the squash halves flesh-side down in a medium baking pan. Add ¼ inch of water to the pan and cover with aluminum foil. Bake until the squash is tender, 35 to 40 minutes. Remove and let cool.

3 When the squash is cool enough to handle, use a fork to scrape the flesh into strands, and place them in a large bowl. Add ½ cup of the marinara. Squeeze out any excess water from the spinach, place in a separate bowl, and add ¼ cup of the Parmesan, the salt (if using), and the cayenne. Mix, making sure the spinach isn't clumped. (I find clean hands are the best tool for this.)

4 Grease a 2-quart baking dish with olive oil. Transfer the squash mixture to the dish. Top evenly with the remaining ¼ cup marinara and sprinkle with the remaining 2 tablespoons Parmesan. Bake for 20 minutes, or until the cheese is browned. Let sit for 10 minutes before serving.

Makes 8 side dish servings

MAKE AHEAD: Roast the squash and remove the strands up to 24 hours ahead; refrigerate.

Nutrition per serving: 100 calories; 4g protein; 3g fat (1g sat. fat); 17g carbohydrates; 4g fiber; 7g sugars; 210mg sodium; 132mg calcium; 1.4mg iron; 387mg potassium; 6mg vitamin C; 4,461IU vitamin A

ONE 2½- TO 3-POUND SPAGHETTI SQUASH

OLIVE OIL

¾ CUP MARINARA SAUCE, HOMEMADE OR HIGH-QUALITY STORE-BOUGHT

ONE 10-OUNCE PACKAGE FROZEN CHOPPED SPINACH, DEFROSTED AND WELL DRAINED

¼ CUP PLUS 2 TABLESPOONS GRATED PARMESAN CHEESE

1 TEASPOON SALT (OPTIONAL)

⅛ TEASPOON CAYENNE PEPPER

BABY LAMB CHOPS
with Lemony Herb Sauce

There is nothing cuter than seeing a baby holding a lamb chop by the bone and gnawing on the tender meat. Serve any leftover sauce dolloped on scrambled eggs or spooned atop roasted veggies.

For the sauce

2 CUPS PACKED TENDER FRESH HERBS, SUCH AS PARSLEY, CILANTRO, MINT, AND/OR BASIL

½ CUP OLIVE OIL

2 TEASPOONS FRESH LEMON JUICE

½ TEASPOON SALT (OPTIONAL)

FRESHLY GROUND BLACK PEPPER

PINCH OF RED PEPPER FLAKES (OPTIONAL)

For the lamb chops

6 BABY LAMB CHOPS, FRENCHED (BONE EXPOSED)

¼ TEASPOON SALT (OPTIONAL)

FRESHLY GROUND BLACK PEPPER

1 TABLESPOON OLIVE OIL

1 Preheat the oven to 400°F.

2 To make the sauce, place all the sauce ingredients in a food processor and process until smooth.

3 To make the lamb, sprinkle the lamb chops with the salt (if using) and pepper to taste. Make sure to season both sides!

4 Heat the olive oil in a large, oven-safe skillet over medium-high heat. Cook the lamb chops until well browned on the first side, about 3 minutes. Flip and transfer the skillet to the oven. Roast for 3 minutes, or until just pink in the middle (thicker lamb chops may need another minute or two).

5 Cool and serve the lamb chops with the sauce for dipping.

Makes 6 lamb chops and ½ cup sauce

MAKE AHEAD: Prepare the sauce up to 24 hours ahead of time. Refrigerate with a thin layer of olive oil on top. Bring to room temperature before serving.

Nutrition per serving (1 lamb chop and 1 tablespoon sauce): 317 calories; 23g protein; 25g fat (6g sat. fat); 1g carbohydrates; 1g fiber; 0g sugars; 102mg sodium; 50mg calcium; 2.6mg iron; 464mg potassium; 24mg vitamin C; 1,494IU vitamin A

Slow-Cooker
MAPLE-DIJON PORK

The slow cooker is genius at turning tough cuts of meat into tender, savory bites perfect for beginning eaters. This recipe couldn't be simpler. Serve on slider buns with a bit of barbecue sauce. Or spoon over polenta or fold into tortillas.

1 Spray a 5-quart slow cooker with nonstick cooking spray.

2 In a small bowl, stir together the maple syrup, Dijon, salt (if using), paprika, and pepper to taste. Rub the pork all over with the maple mixture and place in a slow cooker.

3 Cover the slow cooker and cook on Low for 8 hours.

4 Shred the meat with two forks.

Makes 8 servings

MAKE AHEAD: Refrigerate for up to 3 days.

NONSTICK COOKING SPRAY

1 TABLESPOON MAPLE SYRUP

1 TABLESPOON DIJON MUSTARD

2 TEASPOONS SALT (OPTIONAL)

1 TEASPOON SMOKED PAPRIKA

FRESHLY GROUND BLACK PEPPER

3 POUNDS PORK SHOULDER, SKIN REMOVED

Nutrition per serving: 134 calories; 17g protein; 6g fat (2g sat. fat); 2g carbohydrates; 0g fiber; 2g sugars; 110mg sodium; 14mg calcium; 1mg iron; 295mg potassium; 1mg vitamin C; 5IU vitamin A

Curried
POTATO & BROCCOLI TRIANGLES

These tasty triangles also make excellent lunchbox food.

1 MEDIUM RUSSET POTATO (PEELED AND CUBED)

2 CUPS BROCCOLI FLORETS

1½ TEASPOONS CURRY POWDER

¾ TEASPOON SALT (OPTIONAL)

FRESHLY GROUND BLACK PEPPER

30 WONTON WRAPPERS, DEFROSTED IF FROZEN

1 TABLESPOON PLUS 1 TEASPOON CANOLA OIL

1 Preheat the oven to 375°F. Line two rimmed baking sheets with parchment paper.

2 Place a steamer basket over 1 inch of water in a large saucepan. Bring to a boil over medium-high heat. Add the potato chunks, cover, and steam for 5 minutes. Add the broccoli florets and steam for 5 minutes more, or until both the potatoes and broccoli are tender. Transfer the vegetables to a large bowl.

3 Using a fork or potato masher, mash the broccoli and potatoes until mostly smooth. Stir in the curry powder, salt (if using), and pepper to taste.

4 Lay a wonton wrapper on a clean work surface and set a small bowl of water nearby. Place 2 teaspoons of the potato mixture in the center of the wrapper. Dip your finger in the water and dab the water across the edges of the wonton. Fold one corner of the wonton over to form a triangle and press the edges together with your fingers to seal. Transfer the wonton to the prepared baking sheet and repeat with the remaining wrappers and filling.

5 Brush each wonton with a little canola oil and bake for 12 to 15 minutes, or until golden brown, turning once.

6 Cool and serve whole or cut into pieces. If the corners are especially crispy, break them off before serving to baby.

Makes 30 triangles

Nutrition per serving (1 triangle): 41 calories; 1g protein; 1g fat (0g sat. fat); 7g carbohydrates; 1g fiber; 0g sugars; 49mg sodium; 7mg calcium; 0.4mg iron; 63mg potassium; 3mg vitamin C; 3IU vitamin A

CHEESEBURGER TRIANGLES

Mix up these crowd-pleasers by using Monterey Jack, feta, or Swiss cheese in place of the cheddar.

---

1 TABLESPOON CANOLA OIL, PLUS MORE FOR BRUSHING

½ POUND GROUND BEEF

½ CUP FINELY CHOPPED ONION

½ TEASPOON SALT (OPTIONAL)

FRESHLY GROUND BLACK PEPPER

30 WONTON WRAPPERS, DEFROSTED IF FROZEN

1 CUP SHREDDED CHEDDAR CHEESE (2 OUNCES)

1 Preheat the oven to 375°F. Line two rimmed baking sheets with parchment paper.

2 Heat the canola oil in a large skillet over medium-high heat. Add the ground beef, onion, salt (if using), and pepper to taste. Cook, breaking up the meat with a spoon, until the beef is no longer pink. Drain.

3 Lay a wonton wrapper on a clean work surface and set a small bowl of water nearby. Place 1 to 2 teaspoons of the beef mixture in the center of the wrapper. Add a few strands of grated cheese. Dip your finger in the water and dab the water across the edges of the wonton. Fold one corner of the wonton over to form a triangle and press the edges together with your fingers to seal. Transfer the wonton to the prepared baking sheet and repeat with the remaining wrappers and filling.

4 Brush each wonton with a little canola oil and bake for 12 to 15 minutes, or until golden brown, turning once.

5 Cool and serve whole or cut into pieces. If the corners are especially crispy, break them off before serving to baby.

Makes 30 triangles

Nutrition per serving (1 triangle): 67 calories; 3g protein; 4g fat (2g sat. fat); 5g carbohydrates; 0g fiber; 0g sugars; 74mg sodium; 33mg calcium; 0.5mg iron; 33mg potassium; 0mg vitamin C; 39IU vitamin A

VEGGIE TOFU TRIANGLES

Dinner is especially fun when it's folded into wonton wrappers. If you can't find coleslaw mix, use 3 cups shredded cabbage and 1 cup shredded carrots instead.

1 Preheat the oven to 375°F. Line two rimmed baking sheets with parchment paper.

2 Heat the canola oil in a large skillet over medium heat. Add the coleslaw mix and cook, letting the cabbage wilt, for 4 minutes. Add the soy sauce and tofu, and cook for 1 minute more.

3 Transfer the cabbage mixture to a large cutting board and finely chop.

4 Lay a wonton wrapper on a clean work surface and set a small bowl of water nearby. Place 2 teaspoons of the cabbage mixture in the center of the wrapper. Dip your finger in the water and dab the water across the edges of the wonton. Fold one corner of the wonton over to form a triangle and press the edges together with your fingers to seal. Transfer the wonton to the prepared baking sheet and repeat with the remaining wrappers and filling.

5 Brush each wonton with a little canola oil and bake for 12 to 15 minutes, or until golden brown, turning once.

6 Cool and serve whole or cut into pieces. If the corners are especially crispy, break them off before serving to baby.

Makes 30 triangles

1 TABLESPOON CANOLA OIL, PLUS MORE FOR BRUSHING

8 OUNCES COLESLAW MIX (4 CUPS; SEE HEADNOTE)

1 TABLESPOON REDUCED-SODIUM SOY SAUCE

4 OUNCES EXTRA-FIRM TOFU, CRUMBLED

30 WONTON WRAPPERS, DEFROSTED IF FROZEN

Nutrition per serving (1 triangle): 37 calories; 1g protein; 1g fat (0g sat. fat); 6g carbohydrates; 1g fiber; 1g sugars; 69mg sodium; 15mg calcium; 0.4mg iron; 37mg potassium; 4mg vitamin C; 368IU vitamin A

acknowledgments

A big thank-you to Sharon Bowers, not only a dedicated agent, but also a super-fun lady to drink a negroni with. Thank you for being my partner in this publishing adventure.

I am so grateful to the whole team at Houghton Mifflin Harcourt, especially the always positive and insightful Stephanie Fletcher. It has been a pleasure working with you. Thank you also to Jessica Gilo, Michelle Triant, and Joyce Lin, who are such pros at spreading the word, and to Alissa Faden, whose design of this book and my two previous, under the art direction of Melissa Lotfy, are spot-on perfect.

I couldn't have asked for a better photo team than the trio of creative women who made the images in this book so delightful. Thank you, thank you Lauren Volo, Monica Pierini, and Martha Bernabe. I could have hung out with you for days.

Thank you to all of my friends and colleagues at *Parents*, especially Laura Fenton who said while I was working on a story about baby-led weaning, "Maybe that should be your next book!" Thank you also to Steve Engel and Heidi Reavis, who have been an important part of my life for fifteen years.

Thank you to my friends, who cheer me on with such enthusiasm: Nicole Page, Danielle Wilkie, Allison Graham, Felicity Rowe, Heather Date, Jessica Winchell Morsa, and Grace Bastidas. I am a lucky lady.

One of the true pleasures of having published books is getting to know readers. I am so grateful to all the parents and grandparents who found *Real Baby Food* useful. Your enthusiasm has been inspiring.

Writing about parents feeding children always makes me think of my own parents, of course. Andy and Linda Helwig have been my biggest fans every day of my life. Thank you from the bottom of my heart.

And, last but not least, Dave and Rosa, my two people. Thank you for your patient taste testing, honest feedback, endless good humor, and constant support. Je vous aime.

INDEX

Note: Page references in *italics* indicate photographs.

metric conversion guide

Note: The recipes in this cookbook have not been developed or tested using metric measures.
When converting recipes to metric, some variations in quality may be noted.

MEASUREMENTS

Inches	Centimeters
1	2.5
2	5.0
3	7.5
4	10.0
5	12.5
6	15.0
7	17.5
8	20.5
9	23.0
10	25.5
11	28.0
12	30.5
13	33.0

TEMPERATURES

Fahrenheit	Celsius
32°	0°
212°	100°
250°	120°
275°	140°
300°	150°
325°	160°
350°	180°
375°	190°
400°	200°
425°	220°
450°	230°
475°	240°
500°	260°

VOLUME

U.S. Units	Canadian Metric	Australian Metric
¼ teaspoon	1 mL	1 ml
½ teaspoon	2 mL	2 ml
1 teaspoon	5 mL	5 ml
1 tablespoon	15 mL	20 ml
¼ cup	50 mL	60 ml
⅓ cup	75 mL	80 ml
½ cup	125 mL	125 ml
⅔ cup	150 mL	170 ml
¾ cup	175 mL	190 ml
1 cup	250 mL	250 ml
1 quart	1 liter	1 liter
1½ quarts	1.5 liters	1.5 liters
2 quarts	2 liters	2 liters
2½ quarts	2.5 liters	2.5 liters
3 quarts	3 liters	3 liters
4 quarts	4 liters	4 liters

WEIGHT

U.S. Units	Canadian Metric	Australian Metric
1 ounce	30grams	30 grams
2 ounces	55 grams	60 grams
3 ounces	85 grams	90 grams
4 ounces (¼ pound)	115 grams	125 grams
8 ounces	225 grams	225 grams
16 ounces (1 pound)	455 grams	500 grams
1 pound	455 grams	0.5 kilogram